COMMUNICATION FOR GENDER SENSITIZATION

About the Author

Manisha Pathak Shelat teaches at the Faculty of Journalism and Communication, The Maharaja Sayajirao University of Baroda, India. With over 15 years of professional experience in communication practice, education and research, Dr. Shelat has contributed articles to well known academic and popular journals. She was visiting faculty at the King Mongkut's University of Technology Thonburi, Bangkok, Thailand and has travelled extensively in India and abroad. She received faculty research award of the Shastri Indo-Canadian Institute in 1996 to study the Canadian experience in media literacy. Dr. Shelat has been associated with several organisations as consultant and her special interests include development support communication, media literacy/education, media for children and young people, and gender issues.

COMMUNICATION FOR GENDER SENSITIZATION
The Value Discussion Approach

Manisha Pathak Shelat

CONCEPT PUBLISHING COMPANY, NEW DELHI-110059

ISBN 81-8069-020-2

First Published 2004

Printed and Published by
Ashok Kumar Mittal
Concept Publishing Company
A/15-16, Commercial Block, Mohan Garden
New Delhi-110059 (India)

Phones: 25351460, 25351794

Fax: 091–(11)–25351703

E-mail: publishing@conceptpub.com

For my Parents
Yogini and Chandravadan Pathak

"Giving shape to feelings is tough, words crumble like sand;
But I know, as always they'll understand."

FOREWORD

"Gender refers to the cultural construction of sexual differences". Gender roles are the activities a culture assigns to each sex". Kottak (2002:274)*

In the Constitution of India equality between sexes has been guaranteed as an article. However, the existing cultural differences between the sexes were not reflected leading to serious problems of inequality, which has remained an important issue in India. Dr. Manisha Shelat's current research amply highlights these differences and consequent implications in the Indian society.

Mass media is considered to be an essential means to bring about social change in the democratic societies. Appropriate media use can help achieve gender equality even in the traditional patriarchal societies like India. The book attempts to highlight the positive use of mass media in achieving gender equality.

The present book is an outcome of author's Ph.D. thesis in which Dr. Shelat has used "Value Discussion Model" for bringing about gender equality among the adolescents. In doing so, efforts have been made to evaluate the effectiveness of the two major components of the value discussion model — "dilemma" and "discussion". The book has made an effort to "evaluate the effectiveness of value discussion model in communication for gender equality among adolescents". The focus in her study is attitude, stereotyping, value judgement and value clarification with respect to gender equality among adolescents.

The students of standard 11, generally the age group of 15 to 16 formed the universe of the study. The students were divided

---

* *Cultural Anthropology* (Ninth Edition) by Conrad Phillip Kottak, McGrow Hill (2002).

as experimental group and the other as a control group. While there were 66 students in the experimental group, the control group consisted of 79 students. Both in experimental and control groups attempts were made to keep more or less equal number of males and females, though in the experimental group the ratio of female were higher than males. Using a quasi-experimental design the pre and post-data were collected for the study with the help of a self-administered questionnaire. In addition qualitative data were also collected with the help of a detailed guide.

Based on the analysis only four hypotheses could be rejected out of 24 null hypotheses formulated. In most cases, after the post-test, gender stereotyping reduction was noted.

Dr. Shelat has concluded that adolescent boys and girls found value discussion approach interesting and useful in exploring gender issues. She also found that the Discussion Model was effective in changing gender stereotype and value judgement with respect to gender equality among adolescents.

The author argues that the importance of this study cannot be judged merely from statistics. Statistical anlaysis may or may not show change at conventionally accepted significant level in areas like improvement in attitudes, stereotyping or value judgement. She observed that various options, choices and life styles discussed during the study have shaken absolute and uncritical acceptance of the *status quo* of at least some students. The ideas and questions raised may remain dormant for a long time but would spark-off when the adolescents face a gender related value-conflict.

The observations in this study with respect to the professions of Collector and Police Officer as a result of mass media exposure were interesting. The profession of Police Officer was considered appropriate for both genders but that of Collector was considered more appropriate for men before treatment. After the treatment there was a remarkable shift in case of Collector as profession.

The author has suggested that discussion and mass media, both should make efforts to expose the adolescent to images that counterattack gender stereotyping created by cultural construction of sexual differences.

This book reflects the rigour of research methodolgy employed to study the prevailing gender inequality The study provides an excellent commentary on the existing stereotyping within a cultural region of Gujarat believed to be "progressive" where women enjoy higher status compared to parts of India.

The study will provide new insights to those who are keen to understand existing inequalities between male and female in India.

BINOD C. AGRAWAL
Director,
TALEEM Research Foundation,
City Plaza, Sterling City,
Bopal, Ahmedabad 380 058.

PREFACE

Doctoral research normally takes up considerable time. Mine took me a little more than four years. It helped that I had chosen to work on ideas and issues close to my heart. Gender and Communication. The rest of the book contains ample theoretical discourse on both these core aspects of my work. Here I give a glimpse of the personal.

It is difficult to say when my interest in gender began. Very early, I suppose. It might be a 'congenital defect' as my brother would put it. Observation and questioning of gender related ideas and practices in my immediate surroundings planted the seed.

If we go by the average experience of gender discrimination I have nothing to complain of. As the first-born and only daughter of highly educated parents, I always felt welcome and cherished. My husband's friends and relatives have branded him a 'converted feminist'. I work in a university where equal pay for men and women is the accepted norm and it is common to see women in positions of power. In fact there was a time when the three most powerful posts in the university—that of the Chancellor, the Vice-Chancellor and the Pro-Vice Chancellor were held by women. Also, women in my country never had to fight for their right to vote unlike of many so-called advanced democracies. And yet I can see the undercurrents of socio-cultural gender expectations operating in every major life event and decision of mine—socialization, career choice and development, marriage, life style and responsibilities...However subtle, howsoever invisible, these forces have had powerful impact on the way my life has shaped up. Well, the process of reconciling the 'feminine' and the 'feminist' within has left a few scars on me but there are thousands of girls and women who continue to live with bleeding, unhealed wounds.

I have also met men who have admitted the burden of immense gender pressure. Anyway, I strongly believe that gender issues are not just women's issues; they are human issues and hence men have always been an integral part of my work on gender.

Reading and talking to women and men from different parts of the world enlarged my perspective. It helped me go beyond my limited personal viewpoint and at the same time confirmed the universality of gender myths. I still remember attending a seminar on 'Balancing Work and Family Life' at Massachussetts Institute of Technology way back in 1987. I was naive enough then to be shocked to find not a single man in the audience.

I have not touched upon grave issues like sexual abuse, domestic and public violence, female feticide, reproductive rights, torture and oppression at home and at work places...I wanted to begin with the day-to-day experiences of urban middle class adolescents so that they can strongly relate to the theme under discussion and participate in the debate. Besides, the seemingly mundane issues like sharing the housework have been at the root of many ruined careers, lost opportunities and grave health problems. In India it is such a common sight to see the wife slogging over cooking, kids and housework and the husband not even looking up from the newspaper. Both may have to leave for work at the same time and yet there is not the slightest pang of guilt in the man because it is 'natural' for women to do the housework. An important aspect of my project was to help adolescents explore the illusions and myths generated by confusing the 'cultural' as 'natural'.

Communication plays a significant role in reinforcing and simultaneously reshaping the way we think of us and others as 'men' or 'women'; also in how others perceive us. In the process of molding themselves into 'ideal' or 'desirable' men and women young people keep buried within resentment, doubts, uncertainties and contradictions. Where is the platform where they can voice all these and are not judged or punished for thinking aloud? This was one of the reasons for choosing a participation oriented communication approach. Sensitization is a slow, gradual process that has to evolve from within.The communication channels under dominant paradigm do not have the scope or intention to facilitate this.

I still believe in the classic definition of communication. More than selling ideas, marketing lifestyles, converting audiences or amassing power and mega bucks, communication has to bring people together, bridge the gap between generations, communities, sexes; facilitate sharing of ideas and greater understanding. It has to remain a lifelong process of questioning stereotypes and conventions, exploring the world with all its many splendoured cultures, accepting differences as interesting variations, and cultivating openness and empathy in all relationships.

Unlike what many believe, gender sensitization is not role-reversal, male bashing, or 'trying-to-undo-what-God-has-done'...Balance. Harmony Happiness. These are the ultimate goals of communication for gender sensitization.

I dedicate this book to my infant daughter Revati (who yet doesn't know what it is to be a 'girl') and her generation of boys and girls with a hope that when they become men and women, they will share in true sense the agonies and ecstasies of running the world and home.

MANISHA PATHAK SHELAT

ACKNOWLEDGEMENTS

A large number of friends, colleagues, and experts offered guidance, assistance, and encouragement during the study. Many of them remain unmentioned here but the study owes a lot to their support.

Professor Sneha Joshi, my guide and then Dean, Faculty of Education and Psychology, MSUB has been a constant source of encouragement and advice. Her enthusiasm and belief in gender equality helped channelise the research, and she exercised a right mix of patience and push in steering me through I cannot thank her enough.

Colleagues at the Faculty of Education and Psychology and the Faculty of Journalism and Communication of the M.S. University of Baroda, especially Niti Chopra, have been generously supportive. I received total support from the two schools of Vadodara—Shri Pratap High School and Navyug Vidyalaya—for the entire period of study. I am grateful to the Principals, staff and students of both the schools.

Late Professor M.B. Buch patiently listened to my early ideas and gave suggestions, so did Dr. Binod C. Agrawal, then Head, Social Research Group, Development and Education Communication Unit at Indian Space Research Organization, Ahmedabad. I am indebted to Professor D.N. Sansanwal, Director, Institute of Education at Devi Ahilya Vishva Vidyalaya, Indore who spent hours helping me conceptualize the study and at a later stage giving a rigorous scrutiny to the statistical analysis. Dr. Akhilesh Singh at D.A.V.V., Indore gave me valuable inputs for methodology and references. Thanks are also due to Professor Bert Pelto, consultant with the Population Council for a discussion on qualitative analysis.

My students and the entire extended family have taken keen interest throughout the study. I must mention the contribution of two important men in my life, my father Professor Chandravadan Pathak and my husband Professor Uday Shelat who remained thoroughly involved at every stage, from intellectual exercise to exhaustive legwork and proofreading. My mother Dr. Yogini Pathak has always lent her unconditional no-strings-attached support to all my endeavours. Her contribution in preserving my balance through rough patches has been tremendous.

My gratitude to Minu, my aide at home who facilitated my work by cheerfully shouldering many household chores that otherwise would have fallen on my shoulders because of my gender!

CONTENTS

List of Tables

1

CONCEPTUAL FRAMEWORK

PREAMBLE

Equality is an article of faith in the Indian Constitution and guaranteed by specific articles.

The Preamble to the Constitution of India resolves to secure to all its citizens : Justice — social, economic and political; Liberty of thought, expression, belief, faith and worship; Equality of status and opportunity; and to promote among them all Fraternity assuring the dignity of the individual and the unity of the nation (Basu, 1996).

As the Committee on the Status of Women in India (GOI, 1974) points out in the report "Towards Equality", the constitutional guarantees would lead us to treat equality between sexes as a settled fact, for which no discussion was necessary. But there is still considerable ambiguity and ambivalence in the understanding of the need and implications of equality between sexes.

The truth in these observations is indisputable. Though improvement in the status of women was a pledge made by the Constitution makers and admitted by the Government from the very beginning as one of the major tasks facing the country, women still suffer from considerable bias.

Manifestations of gender bias abound in Indian society in day-to-day experiences, so much so that most of the people accept it as something natural and unobjectionable — nothing worth noticing or questioning.

Laws and policies reflect gender bias and so do media, literature, customs and folk songs. Mythology and religious preachings play a crucial role in maintaining the gender myths and stereotypes. Societal attitudes, discrimination and double standards are the constant reminders of the persisting inequalities crossing the boundaries of time, nations and cultures. Men are also victims of gender bias but problems of women in patriarchal societies are more acute.

Thus, there is a wide gap between what is and what ought to be. This gap can be bridged only if the citizens, especially the future citizens, accept and cultivate gender equality as an essential moral value in society.

COMMUNICATION FOR GENDER EQUALITY

Significance of Communication as a catalyst for social change has long been recognised. Though the concept of development and the paradigms of Communication for Development have undergone major shifts in the last forty years, communication remains a key factor in the transformation of any social group. The effectiveness of communication as a catalyst for social change, however, depends a great deal on the social and political will. In absence of such a will communication can be as effectively used for reinforcing the *status quo*.

Informal day-to-day communication within the family and community largely influences one's perspective of gender. Mass Media, however, have become a crucial influencing factor today. As Ramamurti Committee observed "Efforts by the education system to incorporate a gender perspective and promote women's equality need to be accompanied by intervention in the domain of media as well" (GOI, 1994a).

Gender-bias in Mass Media

A review of various research studies on the media portrayal of women undertaken up to 1980 by Gallagher (1981), however, observes : "a consistent picture emerges from those research studies which have investigated the media's portrayal of women. At the very best, the portrayal is narrow; at worst, it is unrealistic, demeaning and damaging". In another study Gallagher (1983) has observed that the depiction of women in mass media is remarkably consistent throughout the world. Barring media controlled by governments with a strong commitment to social change, the overall picture highlighted the negative features of media treatment of women. These included media underrepresentation of women and women's concerns; the use of women as a commodity in advertising; an ambivalent attitude to women evident in certain stereotyped images in which women exclusively and unalterably are "good" and "pure" or definitely and unchangeably "bad" and "immoral".

Reviewing the multitude of articles and papers on the relationship between women and media on the Indian scene Krishnan and Dighe (1989) mention Joshi Committee* report condemning television's heavy reliance on feature films and film-related programmes, emphasising the middle-class orientation of the programme output and the near-eclipse of working class women. Chandiram and Agrawal (1982) also commented on the asymetrical relationship between men and women on Indian television where the 'wife and other' image was predominant.

Bambawale (1994) conducted a study of women's image as projected on cinema screen. After analysing Hindi films produced between 1982 and 1992 and collecting data from 200 women viewers, the study concluded that woman's image was given the least importance in Hindi films. She emerges without a specific identity (her educational achievement or professional role or self-achieved status are never highlighted) and her ideals and ambitions are directed towards acquiring a husband and worshipping him as God.

Informal observation of media for years by the investigator indicates that many a time brilliant, successful, high achieving women are treated with ridicule or as a 'potential risk' in popular television programmes and films, 'taming of the shrew' remaining a favourite theme. Alternatively, women taking up conventionally male professions like that of a police officer or a gangster are eulogised leaving an impression that only by entering the conventionally male domain women can achieve equality. In fact the effect, if any, of a whole week's public service messages on gender equality can be wiped out by the Doordarshan's weekly dose of commercial Hindi films which unquestionably attract bigger audiences and more attention.

This is not to say that men's portrayal on media is without bias.

* The Working Group on Software for Doordarshan set-up in 1982 popularly known as the Joshi Committee.

But the influence of the women's movement and emergence of Women's Studies as a serious academic discipline have had major contribution in acceleration of research and documentation of women and media. Consequently, little attention has been paid to the stereotype portrayal of masculinity in media.

Lack of gender sensitivity and proper understanding of the subtle nuances of gender bias on part of the people handling the mass media is a major problem.

The March 1996 campaign of the Government of Gujarat for their *'Kunvarbai-nu-Mameru'** scheme is a perfect example of how a communication message intended to benefit women can have a totally opposite effect due to deep-rooted gender bias in the communicator's frame of mind.

The television message on Doordarshan begins with an old Gujarati song '*Dikri to Paarki Thaapan Kahevaay*' — a daughter is somebody else's property entrusted to you temporarily. Her proper place is at her in-laws'. The scheme promises Rs. 5000 to parents belonging to economically backward families at the time of daughter's marriage so that she can go to her in-laws with a respectable sum of money.

Joshi (1986), who studied the participation of women at the higher decision-making levels of Doordarshan, reported that of his respondents, a large number of women felt that increasing the proportion of women employees in the structure would improve programme quality and bring about a more balanced (gender) perspective. But Zoonen (1986) found that the conventional notion, that news content would change if the number of women journalists/producers increased, was not supported by empirical evidence. What Zoonen found could very well apply to Indian situation also because it is illogical to assume that just because a person is a woman she would have more gender sensitivity and would value gender equality more than a man. In fact, the long-term subtle socio-cultural influences by the family, schooling, and community often make women victims of cultural conditioning. It is not uncommon to find women at all levels who are steeped in gender bias.

---

* A popular classic in Gujarati literature in which the poet Premanand portrays a father's agony on not being in a position to fulfil the monetary demands of the in-laws of his daughter.

Considering the fact that the official mass media in India, the All India Radio (AIR) and the Doordarshan reach over 800 million people and adding to that the numerous (33,612 in 1993 out of which 5,316 were in English) newspapers and periodicals published (GOI, 1995), the mainstream media could have significant influence in giving direction to social change. Their contribution in encouraging gender equality, however, seems to have remained negligible.

Educational Approaches and Alternative Communication Media for Gender Equality

Throughout history the socially and politically powerful groups have been effectively using media as well as religious preachings, texts and discourse; social and educational institutions including the family, school and politics; and literature for shaping and reinforcing gender bias and gender stereotypes. It is certainly possible to use all these channels of communication for a reverse goal — that of gender equality and gender role-sharing. In fact, communication and education will have to play a key role in this area because social change in an ancient social fabric cannot happen overnight, nor is it achievable through mere legal measures.

This realisation is clearly reflected in India's National Policy on Education (NPE) and also in the modifications undertaken in 1992 (GOI, 1992a). The policy does not talk about merely equal educational opportunities for women. It views education (formal, nonformal and informal) as an agent of basic change, as an instrument of social engineering which will be used to neutralise the accumulated distortions of the past. Programme of action (GOI, 1992b) under NPE (GOI, 1986), also declares that the electronic, print and traditional media will be used to create a climate for equal opportunities for women and girls. They will play a complementary and supportive role in awareness-generation, dissemination of information and communication.

The NCERT handbook on Training Programme on Methodology of Women's Education (NCERT, 1989) considers the following factors very important for bringing social change in gender roles : Government's priority to women's issues and policy changes; willingness of people and institutions to put them in practice; change in attitudes and prejudices concerning women's role in development; change in reproductive, child-care and auxiliary home responsibilities; and redefining of social roles of men and women to encompass both the public roles and the private sphere of the family.

All these factors have to be reflected in the mass media and other communication channels.

The country paper presented by India at the Fourth World Conference on Women at Beijing in 1995 (GOI, 1994b) in an exclusive section on 'Societal Reorientation, Gender Sensitization and Advocacy' gives an overview of efforts made for communication for gender-just society. Alternative forms which can be ideologically and politically more significant are limited in their reach and find it difficult to compete with the mainstream media. Several initiatives, however, do attempt to intervene directly in the process of social and attitudinal change. They work to correct distortions of existing messages and represent women more authentically and positively. This has been an arduous task given the fact that it is seen as marginal with constraints of limited outreach and finances. Yet for many years now a large number of women's organizations, NGOs and Government departments, not to mention individuals, have consistently attempted to : (i) analyse the sexist content of the various media, (ii) to protest and challenge sexism in the media, and (iii) to create alternatives to sensitise society on women's issues (GOI, 1994b). These efforts include : Analysis of textbooks, self-learning modules (for example, NCERT modules), literacy primers and materials, and publication of literature by feminist publishers (*Kali for Women,* for example), Women's Journals (for example, *Manushi*), establishing media advocacy groups working towards constructive intervention and development of interactive media like songs, posters and street plays by NGOs and women's groups. A few individuals and groups have also attempted communication for gender equality through subtle invasion of the mainstream print and electronic media.

Gender Training and Gender Sensitization

The National Perspective Plan for Women (GOI, 1988b) identifies training as a key strategy in changing social attitudes and biases that seep into policy and programme implementation. Training programmes in the area of gender and development cover a wide range of groups : teachers, government officers, police officers, policy makers, and NGO volunteers. Some programmes aim at introducing gender components in the existing training programmes (e.g. Programmes of the Indian Institute of Management in Government, Trivandrum, and the Water Resource Engineering and Management Institute, Vadodara) while some focus exclusively on gender and development (e.g. DANIDA supported Training Packages for Women's Development, gender sensitization programmes of the National Institute of Rural Development and Gender Awareness and Development Workshops by the Women's Studies Research Centre, and Baroda Citizens Council, both of Vadodara).

Many international bodies like UNIFEM, DANIDA, CIDA, SIDA, NORAD, and Royal Netherlands Agency also provide gender training to their planners and staff and some non-government donor agencies like Oxfam, Action for World Solidarity and Friedrich Neumann Foundation arrange workshops and seminars for their project partners.

The New Communication Paradigm : Participation, Sharing and Analysis

The perspectives concerning the role of communication in development have changed greatly in the 1980s and 1990s.

Describing the paradigm shift in 'Communication for Development', Melkote (1991) emphasises greater participation of the beneficiaries in the development process in general and in message development in particular. "There is a shift from the concept of Development Communication (DC) with its emphasis on top-down, big-media centred, government-to-people communication to Development Support Communication (DSC) focused on co-equal, little-media-centred, government-with-people communication" (Ascroft and Masilela, 1989). A concomitant development is "the emergence of a new development professional : the development support communicator who mediates between the technical experts and their beneficiaries" (Melkote, 1991).

The new paradigm of the 1990s, envisages new functions for communication in development. According to Diaz-Bordenave (1989), some of the new functions for communication media that may contribute significantly to a participative society are :

(i) to help in the development of a community's cultural identity,
(ii) to act as a vehicle for citizen's self-expression,
(iii) to facilitate problem articulation, and
(iv) to serve as tools for diagnosis of community's problems.

Discussing the gender training strategies, the Country Paper (a draft) by India for the Fourth World Conference on Women at Beijing in 1995 also warns against communication modules brought from outside and for a short duration. "Gender training itself is not merely a skill, but the result of conceptual clarity. It is also critical for the success of the effort that it is participatory and that the conclusions are reached through reflection and analysis so that they are internalised" (GOI, 1994b).

Communication for Gender Equality at School Level

The formative school years in an individual's life are very important if gender equality as a value is to be imbibed in the society.

Socialization has far-reaching significance at school level also. Every student brings with him or her a set of gender related attitudes and expectation. Socialization of teachers and its consequences also have significant influence on the gender related attitudes and practices of students. Added to these are attitudes and values of administrators, policy makers and curriculum planners.

To make the matter more complex, children and adolescents form a large portion of consumers of the mainstream media.

With respect to the socialization of the young, Krishnakumar (1986) comments with insight on the role of formal education, more specifically of school in sex-role learning. He challenges the view that the school and community should be complementary to each other in socialising the young : "If one accepts this principle of complementarity, then there is no hope for changing the prevailing code of sex-typing through education, which means that there is no hope that education can intervene in the cultural reproduction of entrenched sex-roles". Reflecting on the ways and means by which the school can act as a counter-socialiser in sex-role learning, Krishnakumar emphasises that when cinema and television cast in conservative images of women and men, the school's media — that is, textbooks and other materials — should offer images and symbols that motivate the reader to look at human beings in terms of their own struggle for an identity rather than as reciting prefabricated conversations. "... If acceptance of the prevailing order and its norms is what society demands, then the school should demand the spirit of inquiry and should offer opportunity to practice it".

Ramamurti Committee also supports this view : "Outmoded traditions and myths that hinder positive development of women and their role in national life should be objectively discussed in the classroom in a gender perspective" (GOI, 1994a).

The communication approach selected for the present study attempts to give students these opportunities as it focuses on participation, sharing, inquiry and analysis.

CONCEPTUAL FRAMEWORK

Gender Equality

To understand the problems of gender bias and to appreciate the philosophy of gender equality it is essential to first understand the words 'Gender' and 'Gender Roles'.

The word 'Gender' is used in grammar to classify words roughly answering to sex (Chamber's, 1972). The terms 'Gender' and 'Sex' are often used interchangeably but the distinction is that 'Sex' is purely biological whereas 'Gender' is constituted biologically, socially, economically, culturally, and above all, politically (McLaren, 1988).

Role is defined as a set of rights, duties and expectations associated with a particular position in the society (Baker *et al.*, 1980). Gender role concerns rights, duties and expectations associated with being a man or a woman. Some writers use the term sex roles when they speak of purely biological functions (such as having babies) or characteristics (such as breast development), and the term 'gender roles' when they mean behaviour that is learned and can be acted out by persons of either biological sex (such as being emotional or cooking).

Gender Equality is a complex concept that does not stay fixed. Though being a constituent of the set of basic democratic values, its definition varies over time, situations, cultures and social groups. If one uses the notion of 'difference' as an organizing principle, one can periodise the entire history of feminism in terms of the domination, in alteration, of an androgynous and a female-uniqueness view of women's subordination and liberation. The eighteenth and early nineteenth century Enlightenment feminists, religious and secular, tended towards an androgynous vision of the fundamental humanity of men and women; that is, they emphasised the artificial imposition of femininity upon women as part of a system subordinating, constricting and controlling them with the result that 'women' as an historically created category, had had their capacities as well as their aspirations reduced. By contrast, the later nineteenth century feminists tended towards a female moral superiority view. They applauded what was different in women, and while they were not always biologistic in their assumptions about how men and women became different, the process of differentiation was less interesting to them than the result : a world divided between a male principle of aggression and a female one of nurturance. Motherhood was the fundamental defining experience of womanhood (Gordon, 1991).

In the second wave of feminism, a similar movement from androgyny to female uniqueness occurred. The early women's liberation movement, both radical and liberal, emphasized equal rights and equal access for women to previously male privilege. In the past decade, we have seen again a celebration of women's unique and superior qualities with, again, an emphasis on mothering as both source and ultimate expression of these qualities. But it is not as if an acute shift occurred from one perspective to another; rather this duality persists continuously within feminism, e.g. on one side, there is a demand for equality in the spheres of career, achievement and wages, which is hardly possible without higher male participation in child rearing, while at the same time 'female superiority' view glorifies the mystical and special bond between mother and child which no other relationship could replicate.

Gender Equality has also become a controversial term over the years. Radical egalitarians claim that man and woman are exactly equal in all respects. This narrow view, apart from being scientifically unsound, has serious consequences. It does not respect the special biological necessities of women for which they need special protection and privileges (e.g. during periods of maternity, lactation etc.). As Hirst (1976) points out "Egalitarianism can never lead to equality. It can only apply an equal standard to qualitatively unequal class."

Before exploring any intervention approach it is important to examine several perspectives and arrive at the perspective for the present study.

Gender Equality : Different Perspectives

Both feminist scholarship and women's studies came, of course, directly out of the women's movement. Feminist scholarship has taken up not simply the task of developing an understanding of the world that takes women into account, it also has as its explicit goal the search for the origins of women's oppression and formulation of effective strategies for change. The subject of Women's Studies was developed primarily as one of the strategies for change. It was seen as a way of disseminating feminist scholarship and of 'educating for change'. The basis of feminist scholarship and of Women's Studies is thus a commitment to social change, specifically addressed to ending the oppression of women (Lowe and Lowe Benston, 1991).

Different groups of women including scholars and activists, however, have different perspectives on 'social change', the concept and nature of equality between men and women and also on strategies and approaches for social change. Thus, there is no universal model to which everyone has to subscribe.

Discussing the perspective taken by different branches of feminism, Lowe and Lowe Benston (1991) emphasise "... it should be recognised not only that labels are imprecise and represent abstractions of real positions but also that most feminists share all of these views to some extent and differ primarily in emphasis."

Liberal Perspective

Liberal feminists ask for equal opportunity to women to compete within the existing system. This branch of feminism is much less committed to egalitarian aims and collective work styles than the others and makes the general assumption that women will act like men given equal opportunity. Attempts at institutional change are directed towards those ideas and institutions that seem to keep women in disadvantaged positions, such as sex-role socialization, inequality of opportunity, unequal access to education, and (female) responsibility for child rearing and housework. The assumption is that women's oppression serves no real social function, so that the institutions seen as specifically oppressive to women can be changed without any fundamental change in other social institutions.

The liberal feminist idea that changes in individual consciousness are the critical factors in eliminating women's oppression has been a strong element in planning educational approaches and in focusing on real legal and social barriers faced by women in our society.

Radical Perspective

Radical feminists argue that the oppression of women is built into the very structure of our society. The division between the sexes based on the patriarchal family is seen as fundamental to social organization. Other hierarchical oppressive social structures are developments that come out of patriarchy. Thus, all such structures must be rejected if women are to be liberated. This branch of feminism sees equality for women within the present system as impossible and calls for a radical restructuring of society, involving the elimination of patriarchy and along with it all other hierarchical structures.

Marxist-Socialist Perspective

The Marxist-Socialist feminists also believe that women's oppression is so deeply rooted that only a basic restructuring of society can change it. This branch of feminism emphasizes the way in which the specific form of women's oppression changes from one society to another and links the position of women to economic and social institutions characteristic of a particular society.

Socialist-feminist theory, relying on both Marxism and structuralism, emphasises the importance of equity between genders in all spheres of activities, traditional and non-traditional, private and public. Liberal perspective on the other hand, emphasises the increasing movement of women into non-traditional role. Socialist-feminists assume that media and popular culture perpetuate and develop cultural ideology, and if women's status is to improve, these structures must change. They further argue that transforming mass media and popular culture can make a difference even in absence of a socialist revolution. In this they differ from Marxist perspective which emphasises that change in women's status is predicated on changes in the economic structure of the state (Steeves, 1986).

Gender Bias : The Male Viewpoint

Most people tend to associate gender oppression with oppression of women. Besides, men often fail to see their problems as related to gender bias because they have been taught that they are the powerful sex. Violating gender roles has often more severe consequences for a male than for a female because when a woman tries to adopt the 'male' ways of behaviour, develop the 'male' qualities or choose a conventionally male domain of work she is viewed as progressing from the 'inferior' to the 'superior' and if she is successful, she gains certain rewards like money, power and independence. But in case of a man who has qualities perceived as feminine or who chooses a conventionally female domain of work, the society views him as regressing to something inferior and the degree of social disapproval and ridicule is greater. Besides, he risks losses in terms of power, prestige, and money.

Brannon and David (1976) interpret the male role in terms of four factors :

(1) No Sissy Stuff : The stigma of anything even vaguely feminine.

(2) The Big Wheel : Success, status, and the need to be looked up to.

(3) The Sturdy Oak : A manly air of toughness, confidence, and self-reliance.

(4) Give 'Em Hell' : The aura of aggression, violence and daring.

In fact some argue that this century's social developments have reduced women's burdens far more than men's burdens and since the advent of feminism women have gained much greater role flexibility and much greater choice between traditional and non-traditional life styles.

Some of the areas where men become victims of gender bias are:

— Overemphasis on achievement,
— Pro-maternal bias in divorce and custody cases,

— Stiffer punishment compared to girls in schools and at home for the same behaviour,
— Overemphasis on women's reproductive rights and men's responsibility for child support, and
— Fabricated charges of spouse abuse, sexual abuse and family violence.

As Young (1994) puts it, "The interest in men's issues is a much-needed corrective to the increasingly obsessive tendency to focus on real or fictitious disadvantages affecting females and ignore those affecting males. Moreover, by encouraging more role-flexibility for men as well as women, and in particular greater male involvement in home life, the men's movement may be an essential step in achieving the work/family balance often described as the key issue on the women's agenda. ..... perhaps the ultimate lesson we have still to learn is that most gender issues are women's and men's issues."

The Concept of Equity

Distributive justice is an important concept for many of the contemporary social issues involving value conflict. In his analysis of justice, Piaget distinguishes two types of distributive justice : equality and equity (Wrightsman, 1977). As explained by Wrightsman, Equality has the same meaning in Piaget's system that it does for most of us: everyone should be treated the same. Equity allows for consideration of individual circumstances; here equality is never defined without taking into account the way that each individual is situated.

The Concept of Androgyny

Treating masculinity and femininity as psychological concepts, Sandra Bem (1975) offered the concept of androgyny to label the possession of approximately equal portions of masculine and feminine characteristics. Androgynous individuals would be those persons who considered themselves to have an equal number of masculine characteristics and feminine characteristics. Bem argues that the most well-developed individual is the one who combines the best of both worlds and who can therefore respond to a greater variety of situations with appropriate behaviour. Androgynous people are basically more adaptive to their environment. The concept of *Ardhanaranarishvara* in Indian mythology corresponds to androgyny.

Using a similar concept of androgyny, Spence *et al.* (1975) have found that those individuals who possess high degrees of both masculine and feminine characteristics possess more self-esteem than do more traditionally sex-typed individuals.

Gender Equality : Perspective of the Present Study

On exploring the various perspectives on gender equality one realises the enormous complexity of the concept. For a balanced, holistic concept of gender equality one has to consider biological factors as well as the constantly changing dynamic nature of society. One has to consciously stay away from the tendency to confuse the 'cultural' with 'natural' and learn to critically examine the roles of biological differences and socio-cultural factors, especially social learning/social education and social structure.

Again, the different perspectives offer a wide range of choices in pursuing the goal of equality and social change. One can take the female superiority view, and strive to transform the entire social system — the values, institutions and the relationships — according to the women's vision of the world. Or one can ignore the inherent biases in the social system and strive to get better deal and more power for women without transforming the society. One can take the male superiority view and try to improve women's situation so that it resembles men's situation; or one can hold on to the 'biology is destiny' theory and shun all attempts at social change. Alternatively, one can recognise the biological differences in men and women and yet believe that it is possible to work towards a more equitable relationship.

For the present study the perspective *vis-a-vis* Gender Equality will have to sharply focus on what exactly is 'essential' for an adolescent boy or a girl of standard 11 to understand about gender and equality. One has also to work within the socio-cultural milieu of the adolescents and the structural boundaries of the school system which makes it imperative that the researcher's approach be more pragmatic than utopian.

Considering all these factors, an effort has been made in the present study to redefine the equation between man and woman which would reflect the respect for democratic values like individual dignity, social justice and equity.

Following are the guidelines followed in the present study to conceptualise gender equality as a value :

(1) Both, men and women, are critical elements in gender issues.

(2) Men and women are different in many ways but different does not always mean superior or inferior. Men and women can be different yet equal if nothing is considered inferior or superior just because it is associated with a particular gender. It is essential to take gender into consideration where it is necessary (e.g. protection for maternity).

(3) Role reversal or "oppressed imitating the oppressor" cannot be an alternative to role stereotype. Role sharing which considers individual differences among men and among women, family needs and biological as well as socio-cultural-economic factors offers a better alternative.

(4) Equality is possible only through mutuality between sexes when in any given sphere (e.g. economic or sexual gratification) no one sex is always a giver and no one sex always a receiver.

(5) Considering the realities of the Indian socio-cultural situation, social change has to be gradual and should come from within over a period of time.

One can begin the process taking a pragmatic approach. To imbibe gender equality as a moral value in the society, however, is a very complex process because of the complexity of the concept of gender equality as well as the complexities in the Value Development Process. Yet, it is essential for a democratic society like India, and can be achieved only through communication and education in the right direction.

Values and Value Development

The basic moral value that undergirds and sustains a democracy is the principle of individual dignity. The individual deserves consideration by virtue of his or her humanness, apart from considerations of wealth, race, sex, or physical or intellectual ability (Hersh, 1980).

Gender Equality, therefore, is an important value for a country like India, which ideologically supports basic democratic values like social justice, individual dignity, freedom of speech and religion and equal protection under the law.

Democracy places heavy demands on the moral capacities of the individual. It requires the individual to make informed judgements about personal interests and the welfare of the community. Ideally, these judgements are based on our values. Values are guides to our behaviour and give focus to life.

Among the three most important categories of values that enter into the activity of teaching are aesthetic values, instrumental values, and moral values (Shaver and Williams, 1976). Aesthetic values are those standards by which we judge beauty. Instrumental values are standards set in order to achieve other standards designed to serve larger ends. Moral values are the standards, the principles by which we judge whether aims or actions are proper. Gender Equality as a value belongs to this third category.

Thus, moral values express something more than a purely individual standard though in the simplest terms value refers to objects that human beings cherish and desire and also consider as desirable. As Shaver and Williams (1976) point out, "Because moral values are used to justify and judge ethical decisions, and these have impact on other people, moral standards are not merely matters of personal taste. Unlike aesthetic or instrumental values, moral values necessarily carry a basic message of obligation." And therefore, moral values are given higher priority in value education.

But value education, certainly, is not an easy task. Value Development is a very complex process. According to Dewey (1939), children learn moral values from the quality of their total social experience. Again, morality depends on the combination of humane caring, objective thinking, and determined action. If any of the three elements is lacking the process remains incomplete. During the process of value development, several inputs work simultaneously : experience, modelling, direct preaching and teaching, intellectualising and reasoning, understanding, appreciating and reacting emotionally.

Another factor that adds to the complexity of Value Development is the fact that our values are not isolated from one another. They are interlocking parts of total value-networks, rather than self-contained units. Hence, value conflict emerges as an essential part of Value Development process. For example, we may value liberty as well as equality but in fulfilling the claims of equality we may have to compromise on liberty and *vice-versa*.

In our daily life we encounter many situations which demand decision making in difficult situations. Ideally, we would make our life choices based on our values and resolve the value conflicts by rational balancing, but in reality it is not all that simple. Many a time we are not clear about our own values. Many of our values are unconscious. Many of us have hardly ever given a thought as to why we cherish a particular value, how we came to cherishing it and what effect that has on our other values and on other people.

Children, youths and adults — all face value conflicts in their life but adolescence is the stage of life when value conflicts are at their peak. We cannot leave their value conflicts unresolved because they are the future citizens, the future policy makers, workforce and homemakers. A well-defined value system is also important for their personal well-being.

Adolescents and Value Conflict

Adolescence (the period between 12 to 19 years) involves accomplishment of a number of critically important developmental tasks. These are : adjustment to the physical changes of puberty and later of adolescent growth and to the flood of new subjective impulses brought on by genital maturity; development of independence from parents or other caretakers; establishment of effective social and working relationships with peers of the same and opposite sex, preparation for a vocation and the development of a system of values and a sense of identity . . . (Conger, 1977).

The development of independence and a philosophy of life based on a consistent value system are very crucial for adolescents but the complexity of the contemporary society has made these tasks increasingly difficult.

Compared to the previous generations, today's adolescents have many more influences on their life. Yesterday's adolescents derived their values from three major sources : family, a relatively homogeneous neighbourhood and a highly structured and moralistic school-programme. Today, concepts of family, neighbourhood and school have undergone major transformation providing a bewildering range of alternatives. Besides, the explosion of oral, written and electronic media has exposed today's adolescents to a variety of cultures and life-styles and to people with paradoxical values and philosophies.

Thus, the multiplicity of sources as well as channels of Value Development offers so many conflicting and confusing possibilities and choices that an adolescent gets bewildered as to how one should arrive at one's own set of values. The value-confusion and conflicts are especially acute in gender related values because gender is constituted biologically, psychologically, socially, economically, culturally and politically and influences most of the life-experiences of a person.

Some of the questions constantly being raised by young people are : Who should be their models? Who is right? How could one balance between the traditions and change, self-interest and social justice? It is difficult and yet essential for young people to find convincing answers to these questions.

Approaches to Value Education

Kirschenbaum (1978) discusses four approaches to help young people find answers to value conflicts : moralising, modelling, *laissez faire* approach and value-clarification approach.

Moralising is increasingly becoming a less preferred approach and in certain cases less effective because in today's society there is no complete consistency about what constitutes 'desirable' values. Though Sommers (1994) criticises the sense of moral relativism pervasive among American students and argues that value educators should make clear distinction between "basic" ethics and "dilemma" ethics. She maintains that as far as universal basic ethics and private morality (virtues) are concerned school children must be taught right from wrong.

Modelling too is rapidly losing its earlier place. The problem is that young people are exposed to too many — and at times, contradictory — models to emulate. Also moralising and modelling, if used as the sole approach to value education, do not give a young person an opportunity to develop his/her own sense of identity, and learn to relate to people whose values differ from his/her own.

The rationale behind the *laissez faire* attitude is that no one value system is right for everyone, so let children decide what they want without intervention in anyway and eventually everything will turn outright. But as Kirschenbaum (1978) points out, everything does not usually turn out all-right. Most young people do not need adults running their lives for them, but they do want and need help.

Value-clarification approach has been one of the more favoured approaches to value education. Raths (1966 and 1967) built upon the thinking of pioneer educational philosopher John Dewey and developed a systematic approach to help students become aware of the beliefs and behaviours they prize and would be willing to stand up for. This approach helps students answer value-related questions, make their own choices, evaluate the consequences and build their own value system. Value clarification approach maintains the principle that the teacher should never directly tell students about right and wrong.

Sommers (1994) has rightly criticised the tendency of value clarification approach to treat one's preference for basic values like honesty or respect for human dignity as one treats one's preference for vanilla over chocolate flavoured ice-cream. She questions the value clarification proponents' tendency to place the locus of moral authority in the individual's private tastes and preferences. Nevertheless, many value clarification techniques provide students with opportunities for the practice of moral reasoning in issues involving broader social perspective.

Value clarification approach uses several techniques like Value Love List, Value Action, Value Voting, Value Ranking, Value Continuum, Incomplete Value Sentences, Coat of Arms, Value Thought Sheet, Value Autobiography, Value Clarification Journal, Value Questions, Value Interview, Value Brainstorming, Value Problem Solving, Value Indicators, Life Raft, Value Role Play, Conversion of Limitations, Fantasy Exploration, Negotiation and Expectation, and Life Process : A Structured Fantasy (Smith, 1977).

'Dilemma' is one of the frequently used techniques in value clarification.

Dilemma as a Pedagogic Tool

Use of Dilemma-based techniques in education, especially moral education, is not new. Way back in 1960s Piaget initiated the approach of confronting a child with stories that pose a moral dilemma. Later Kohlberg extended Piaget's basic theory and developed dilemmas of greater complexity to study different levels and stages in moral development. The dilemmas posed in stories used by Piaget and Kohlberg seek to measure moral judgement or the moral attitudes that determine how a person feels one should respond to acertain situation (Wrightsman, 1977). Carol Gilligan, a former student of Kohlberg, added a gender dimension to the study of moral development. Kohlberg had not included any girls in his studies spanning over 20 years. Gilligan has also used dilemmas and has found interesting differences between boys and girls in their approach to a moral problem (Kohlberg and Giligan, 1971).

Dilemma-based educational approach has been adopted in the school and college level ethics courses all over the United States of America.

Conscientization

Brazilian educator Paulo Freire (1971) first introduced the concept of conscientization which has had profound impact on movement for gender equality.

Freire's disappointment with educational system in Brazil and Chile coupled with his conviction, that 'every human being, no matter how important or submerged in the culture of silence' he may be, is capable of looking critically at his world in a dialogical encounter with others, led him to advocate an alternative. As Shaull (1972) explains, "provided with proper tools for such an encounter a human being can gradually perceive his personal and social reality as well as the contradictions in it, and become conscious of his own perception of that reality and deal critically with it. In this process, the old, paternalistic teacher-student relationship is overcome."

In his most acclaimed and frequently cited work 'Pedagogy of the Oppressed', Freire (1972) has laid down his vision and experiences related to this alternative which came to be known as Pedagogy of Liberation or Critical Pedagogy.

According to Freire, Education with conventional teacher-student relationship suffered from 'narration sickness'. "Narration (with the teacher as narrator) leads the students to memorize mechanically the narrated content. Worse still, it turns them into 'containers', into receptacles to be filled by the teacher."

Freire designated this as the 'banking concept of education'. Advancing the concept of dialogics : the essence of education as the practice of freedom, Freire argued that in the pedagogical system he proposed, the receiver would be liberated from his/her mental inertia, penetrate the ideological mist imposed by the elites and perceive the realities of his/her existence. He called this process conscientization.

Feminist educators often cite Freire as the educational theorist who comes closest to the approach and goals of feminist pedagogy.

> ". . . . Like Freirean pedagogy, feminist pedagogy is grounded in a vision of social change. And like Freirean pedagogy, feminist pedagogy rests on truth, claims of the primacy of experience and consciousness that are grounded in historically situated social change movements. . . . Feminist theory, influenced by post-modernist and cultural identity theories, like other contemporary approaches validates difference, challenges universal claims to truth and seeks to create social transformation in a world of shifting and uncertain meanings" (Weiner, 1991).

Freire used a photograph, a picture or a drawing to represent the existing reality. A discussion was then initiated which sought to conduct an autopsy of the existing realities and encouraged the participants to question why things were as they were, what could be done to rectify the situation, etc. In other words, communication channels were used in this approach to generate a dialogue, to help people talk together and understand each other. Communication was thus a vehicle for liberation from mental and psychological shackles that bound peasants to their existing situations. In many ways communication was performing its true function : 'Communicare' or build commonness (Melkote, 1991).

Value Discussion Model

Value Discussion Model is developed in India by Sansanwal on the principles of value-clarification approach (Singh, 1991). Dilemma and Discussion are the two major components of this model which gives students opportunities to intellectually and frankly discuss among themselves their value-conflicts. It brings into focus their daily experiences and helps them examine individual experiences in wider social context.

Value Discussion model seems to be a suitable approach to discuss gender values with adolescents from two points of view : One, it does not impose any value on youngsters; it encourages thinking and analysis in the right direction and let individuals make their own decisions, it gives students an opportunity to listen to others' reasoning and point-of-view and find out how rational and fact-based are their justifications for their own choices. The present educational system with its emphasis on rote-learning and academic competition does not encourage this kind of independent thinking which is so crucial for adolescents. Two, Value Discussion Model is age appropriate considering the stages in cognitive development. During adolescence a shift occurs in the direction of formal operations. In Piaget's view, the most basic capabilities aimed at during this stage involve a shift of emphasis in the adolescents' thought from the 'REAL' to the 'POSSIBLE'. This is the stage when the child can perform abstract tasks. Here the mode of problem solving is hypothetico-deductive. The educational objective is to train the child in solving abstract problems (Passi *et al.*, 1986).

As Elkind (1971) explains, it is at this point of post-conventional stages of moral development that the adolescent may no longer be able to adopt without question the social or political beliefs of his or her parents.

In Conger's (1977) view adolescence is a period of increasing ability to consider hypothetical possibilities and reason about one's own thought objectively. The adolescent boy or girl, guided by self-awareness, is likely to become more introspective and analytical.

For believing in a value like gender equality in a predominantly patriarchal society, one needs to undertake analysis, questioning and critical thinking beyond what one has learnt from one's own family.

RATIONALE OF THE STUDY

The review of literature, e.g. Verma and Kapadia (1987) and Nuna (1990), shows abundance of studies describing the present status as well as social and educational scenario *vis-a-vis* gender bias and low status of women. Factors affecting the status of women are also discussed by many studies adopting a survey method in most cases. These studies call for action and educational efforts to bring positive change in the existing situation. The report of the National Seminar on Education for Women's Equality (GOI, 1985b and 1988a), United Nations (1975), National Seminar on Education for Women's Equality (GOI, 1985b and 1988a), The National Perspective Plan for Women, 1988-2000 A.D. (GOI, 1988b) and the UGC Guidelines for Development of Women's Studies (UGC, 1982) have all unanimously recommended that communication and education should strike at the deep-rooted attitudes and gender-bias. The present study takes off from this point and reflects the growing concern of researchers to use research for not just reporting the *status quo* or change but also for initiating change.

If the existing patriarchal paradigm of the family and resulting patriarchal constructions of masculinity and femininity have to give way to mutuality, reciprocity, harmony and nurturance in the family, the right attitudes and values have to be nurtured from the young age. Flexible role-sharing brings forth unlimited possibilities and enhances individual and national development but unless people are prepared and trained to take up the dual role and appreciate differences between and also within genders, gender equality would remain just another utopian dream. Today's children are tomorrow's teachers, policy planners, administrators, professionals, spouses and parents. It would be highly undesirable if our future human resources continue to grow up with gender bias, myths and stereotypes without critically thinking about them.

The Non-aligned Ministers' Conference on Role of Women in Development held in New Delhi in 1985 (GOI, 1985a) endorsed that "Structurally, pedagogically and philosophically educational institutions need to play a far more active role in the development of new cultural ethos that can contribute to the realization of the goals of comprehensive development of human material. This also requires that they internalise the concerns for the equality of women and the enhancement of their role in their curricula, pedagogic method, organization and research agendas".

The National Policy on Education (NPE) envisages education as a strategy for achieving a basic change in the status of women (GOI, 1992a, 1992b). NPE's vision for the national education system is to play a positive interventionist role in the empowerment of women and contribute towards development of new values through redesigned curricula and textbooks. There is a strong emphasis that education must address the structures and attitudes that have prevented women's equality till now and have perpetuated and strengthened patriarchal values and institutions that subordinate women. Education must also play an active role in promoting the new values of equality in the division of roles, rights and responsibilities between men and women in every sphere.

If Value Discussion Model emerges as an effective approach for gender-equality communication, it can be included in gender sensitization programmes at school level. Later the model can be adapted for mass media like newspapers and television. It could be tried out with other groups like teachers, parents and policy planners combined with other approaches in action programmes.

STATEMENT OF THE PROBLEM

To study the Effectiveness of Value Discussion Model in communication for gender equality among adolescents.

OBJECTIVES OF THE PRESENT STUDY

(1) To study the effectiveness of Value Discussion Model in terms of change in—

- — attitude towards gender equality
- — gender stereotyping
- — value judgement with respect to gender equality
- — value clarification with respect to gender equality.

(2) To study the influence of sex of the subject, profession of mother, profession of father, education of mother, education of father, and type of family on effectiveness of Value Discussion Model in terms of change in

- — attitude towards gender equality
- — gender stereotyping
- — value judgement with respect to gender equality.

(Only qualitative observations were made in case of Value

Clarification with respect to gender equality.)

DELIMITATIONS OF THE STUDY

(1) The study was delimited to the eleventh (XI) standard students of General Stream of two selected Gujarati medium schools of the city of Vadodara under the Higher Secondary Education Board, Gujarat State.

(2) The period of treatment was delimited to 16 dilemma sessions over a period of four months.

OPERATIONAL DEFINITIONS

Gender Equality

Equality between males and females, allowing consideration of individual circumstances.

Values

The standards/principles by which people judge whether aims/ actions are proper. Values also refer to objects that human-beings cherish and desire and also consider desirable.

Value Discussion Model

It is a model developed in India by Sansanwal in 1986 on the principles of Value Clarification Approach. Dilemma and Discussion are the two major components of this model.

HYPOTHESES OF THE STUDY

Since the study followed experimental design in which hypotheses required statistical testing, they are presented here in the form of null hypothesis :

(1) There will be no significant difference between adjusted mean attitude-towards-gender-equality scores of the control group and those of the experimental group.

(2) There will be no significant difference between adjusted mean gender-stereotype scores of the control group and those of the experimental group.

(3) There will be no significant difference between adjusted mean

value-judgement scores of the control group and those of the experimental group.

(4) There will be no significant difference between the pre-test and post-test scores of attitude towards gender equality in the experimental group.

(5) There will be no significant difference between the pre-test and post-test gender-stereotype scores in the experimental group.

(6) There will be no significant difference between the pre-test and post-test value-judgement scores in the experimental group.

(7) There will be no significant difference in the adjusted mean attitude-towards-gender-equality scores of males and females in the experimental group.

(8) There will be no significant difference in the adjusted mean gender-stereotype scores of males and females in the experimental group.

(9) There will be no significant difference between adjusted mean value-judgement scores of males and females in the experimental group.

(10) There will be no significant difference between adjusted mean attitude-towards-gender-equality scores of children of housewives and those of working mothers in the experimental group.

(11) There will be no significant difference between adjusted mean gender-stereotype scores of children of housewives and those of working mothers in the experimental group.

(12) There will be no significant difference between adjusted mean value-judgement scores of children of housewives and those of working mothers in the experimental group.

(13) There will be no significant difference between the adjusted mean attitude-towards-gender-equality scores of students whose fathers belonged to different professional categories in the experimental group.

(14) There will be no significant difference between the adjusted mean gender-stereotype scores of students whose fathers belonged to different professional categories in the experimental group.

(15) There will be no significant difference between the adjusted mean value-judgement scores of students whose fathers belonged to different professional categories in the experimental group.

(16) There will be no significant difference between the adjusted mean

attitude-towards-gender-equality scores of students whose mothers had different levels of education in the experimental group.

(17) There will be no significant difference between the adjusted mean gender-stereotype scores of students whose mothers had different levels of education in the experimental group.

(18) There will be no significant difference between the adjusted mean value-judgement scores of students whose mothers had different levels of education in the experimental group.

(19) There will be no significant difference between the adjusted mean attitude-towards-gender-equality scores of students whose fathers had different levels of education in the experimental group.

(20) There will be no significant difference between the adjusted mean gender-stereotype scores of students whose fathers had different levels of education in the experimental group.

(21) There will be no significant difference between the adjusted mean value-judgement scores of students whose fathers had different levels of education in the experimental group.

(22) There will be no significant difference between the adjusted mean attitude-towards-gender-equality scores of students from joint families and those from nuclear families in the experimental group.

(23) There will be no significant difference between the adjusted mean gender-stereotype scores of students from joint families and those from nuclear families in the experimental group.

(24) There will be no significant difference between adjusted mean value-judgement scores of students from joint families and those from nuclear families.

2

REVIEW OF LITERATURE

The introduction to the theme, conceptual framework, rationale of the study, objectives and hypotheses have been covered in Chapter 1. The present chapter is devoted to the review of related research.

Because of the interdisciplinary nature of the study encompassing communication, value education and gender sensitization, the literature reviewed was diversified in its content and format.

The studies reviewed are grouped under two major categories: (i) Gender and Communication, and (ii) Value Education.

GENDER AND COMMUNICATION

Studies related to gender and communication encompass a very wide range with widely different concerns, methodology and populations. There is an abundance of studies and surveys describing the present scenario *vis-a-vis* gender bias and low status of women in different fields. The present review, however, is limited to only those studies that include an aspect of communication/educational intervention or are relevant from the point of view of research design and methodology.

Short (1993)'s study "Sex-typed Behaviour in the Primary School : the Significance of Contrasting Explanations" was concerned with explanations of sex-typed behaviour in primary school children. The first was in terms of social pressures to conform to the norms of society. The second focused on children's intellectual commitment to the 'truth' of gender stereotypes, whilst the third was an amalgam of the first two.

To explore children's beliefs about the validity of gender stereotypes, three moral dilemmas were presented to 161 six to eleven year olds. Each dilemma involved an act of discrimination based on a gender stereotype. The children were required to say whether they thought the discriminatory act was fair and to give reasons for their answer.

The study observed that judging by the prevalence of sex-typed behaviour amongst primary-age children, it would seem that many of them lack the courage of their convictions; they actively participate in discriminatory sexist behaviour, despite their beliefs. The study pointed out the need for anti-sexist interventions to acknowledge that a purely cognitive approach to the prevention of gender-based discrimination, whilst necessary for its elimination, is not sufficient. Some children, at least, will also need help in resisting those social pressures that can lead to unfair discrimination. Yet the means of teaching children to withstand these pressures would seem to be an issue that has so far escaped the attention of educationists and others concerned with advancing social justice.

Keefer (1995) in a study entitled "Gilligan's Moral Orientation and Deliberation" focused on the psychology of moral reasoning and in particular on Carol Gilligan's gender-based claim that there are two different orientation to the construal and resolution of moral problems.

The purpose of the research was to advance and test an alternative to Gilligan's gender-based theory of moral reasoning. The proposal offered was that moral reasoning involves the application of a set of norms or rules containing "all things being equal" clauses. If these conditions are assumed to be met the rule or norm excludes considerations of other concerns.

Gender differences were examined in two studies using hypothetical dilemmas. Findings contradicted Gilligan's claim that gender differences are to be found in the form of reasoning; rather, they suggested that while the genders differed in their judgements as to which rules or norms may be treated as exclusionary, once adopted, rules and norms are applied in similar ways. The study argued that Gilligan's contribution to moral theory is not simply that women be included in the moral theory, but that the moral theory itself must include the strategy of reasoning that she found to characterise women's responses to moral conflicts.

Kolia (1995)'s study of gender training programmes used internationally with a focus on African experience aimed to further develop the knowledge base of the field by providing a quantitative analysis of 36 programmes (and their supporting materials) and to describe the state of the art of gender training programme on an international scale. In addition two detailed case studies of gender training programme in African region were presented and analyzed.

Gender training programmes have emerged as important tools to be used in the process of gender sensitization and gender responsiveness in international development and policy. The study documented several interesting findings some of which were : (1) Gender training is taking place in many parts of the world, within various institutions; (2) Equity and efficiency are parallel themes underlying most training programmes; (3) History, tradition and culture play an important role in the oppression of women in the region and are very significant obstacles to the advancement of women in Africa; (4) Collaboration and networking are the keys to progress in the field; (5) Starting with a policy commitment for gender responsiveness from people in power is a useful but not sufficient basis for change; (6) Third World women are active creators of change, but there is a need to develop a critical mass of gender-responsive people in any society; (7) An integrated interactive approach to policy and planning appears to yield a better result as opposed to a linear one; (8) Although the objectives of gender sensitivity and empowerment are being achieved by most training efforts, there is still much work to be done regarding the implementation of the training or the skills learned from it.

The study recommended gender responsive training as an alternate tool to address gender biases.

Gender Balancing the Curriculum : "Attitudes, Knowledge of Feminist Issues and Self-Efficacy of Female Under-Graduates" was the title of a study by Mulvihill (1994) which tested whether it would be feasible to improve attitudes towards women, knowledge of Feminist Issues and Self-Efficacy by gender balancing the curriculum and including same sex role models in the management classes of an undergraduate business school. Subjects participated in an experiment which took place over the course of a college semester. The experiment consisted of a pre-test, post-test and a gender balanced management curriculum.

Subjects in the study were 86 female undergraduates in eight management classes. Four of the classes were randomly assigned to the experimental treatment and four to the control treatment. Two classes in each group had female professors and two had male professors. The curriculum was gender balanced by incorporating in the programme readings and case studies which highlighted women in business in positions of power and authority with decision-making responsibilities, by having female role-models as teachers and guest speakers and through the use of videos highlighting women with successful business careers.

Results of the statistical analysis revealed that attitudes towards women and self-efficacy among female students could be improved significantly by gender balancing the curriculum and including female role models. However, the study failed to support the hypothesis that knowledge of feminist issues could be improved by such modification but indicated that the consciousness was raised in the area.

O'Donnel (1995) conducted an experiment to study the influence of non-traditional books on children's gender stereotypes about adult occupations and on their occupational role-playing with peers. Also of interest was how well children's attitudes match their behaviours relative to gender stereotypes.

Thirty-two four-to-five year olds were randomly assigned to one of eight play groups (four treatment, four control). They were individually questioned concerning adult occupations on four separate occasions (week 2, 3, 4 and 14). At times 3 and 4, prior to measuring, children in the treatment condition were read non-traditional books while those in control condition were read traditional books.

The findings did not support the major hypothesis that children in the treatment group, but not those in the control group, would become less gender stereotypical about adult occupations over time. In addition, this research did not find that boys were more stereotypical than girls. Children were more stereotypical about boys being nurses than about girls being doctors. In general, children's role play was stereotypical regardless of their gender stereotyped attitudes. That is, some children whose beliefs were high on gender stereotyping played non-traditional roles and *vice versa*. Finally, boys were less willing to take on gender non-traditional roles during play than were girls.

The goal of the study entitled "Gender Equity and Schools: Theory and Practice" by Engelberg (1995) was to integrate theoretical writing of modern feminism, critical theory and post-modernism with empirical findings. The study begins with a theoretical analysis of the debate between advocates of critical theory, post-modernism, and feminism. Critical theory tends towards abstraction in its search for utopian ideals of justice, truth, liberation, dialogue and political transformation. Post-modernism rejects "master" narratives and universalising and seeks local and partial truths which reveal the power of patriarchy in the control of knowledge and science. Post-modernism also searches for local centres of resistance but includes the decentred self and the death of theory, which most feminists reject. Feminists are divided : some support critical theory, some support post-modernism and some see merit in both critical theory belief in transformation and the post-modernist belief in challenging the accepted tenets of science, identity and universal truths.

The empirical methods used were qualitative and quantitative observations of 43 classes in a high school. Two surveys about classroom attitudes were conducted : a survey of three senior psychology classes and a survey of ninth and twelfth grade students in a variety of subjects. The results often contradicted the claim of the American Association of University Women's report that girls were short-changed. Girls and boys were sometimes short-changed by tracking or other classroom practices. Class participation does not always reflect achievement. The conclusion suggested that in line with critical feminist theory, schools must find ways of transforming education and social attitudes to make them more equitable.

STUDIES IN THE AREA OF VALUE EDUCATION

A sizeable number of studies have been conducted in the area of Value Education. A greater number of earlier studies were conducted abroad but during the eighties and later several Indian studies have also been conducted. The review includes only those studies which were conducted with adolescents — secondary school students and undergraduates. Studies which had relevance from the methodological point of view are also reviewed.

Kaufman (1974) compared the effectiveness of (i) group career counselling (a credit class) that employed a combination of value clarification, decision making, and career exploration activities, (ii) one-to-one career counselling and (iii) no intervention. The study was conducted with undergraduate junior and senior women and it found that both experimental groups did significantly better than the control group and the value clarification group produced significantly better results than the one-to-one counselling with respect to self-knowledge, knowledge of self in relation to career and planning activities in seeking career information.

Pracejus (1975) conducted an experiment with two groups of eighth graders. One group participated in twelve sessions of discussing stories using a value clarification approach while the other group read the same stories and followed the discussion approach suggested by the publisher. Gains in reading comprehension were compared and the value clarification group was found to have significantly higher reading comprehension compared to the other group.

Rutowski (1975) studied the effect of value clarification, strategies and 'value level' treatment of subject matter on attitude towards science. High school chemistry students formed the sample and were used as their own controls. An attitude test was administered four times before beginning the experimental treatment and four times during it. The increase reached statistical significance on the last attitude test administered. The study concluded that the value clarification strategies and value level treatment of subject matter had a positive effect on students attitude towards science.

Blokker, Glaser and Kirschenbaum (1976) conducted a study titled 'All About Me' using value clarification approach. 250 boys and 250 girls participated in the study. The treatment was administered for five weeks at the rate of one hour per day. It was found that decision making ability improved and the treatment was helpful in their personal control over their own lives.

Morton (1976) conducted a study which used moral dilemmas for the development of moral reasoning. The experiment was carried out with three groups of high school juniors. Each group consisted of 15 students. Experimental Group I participated in discussion of moral dilemmas and also experienced value clarification interventions. Experimental Group II participated only in dilemma discussion session while the Control group was engaged in its normal activities. The study found that the experimental curriculum had a significant effect on overall moral reasoning development.

Hobster (1980) conducted a study to determine the effectiveness of value clarification group activities on the development of student values and value system in young adolescents. Four groups comprising of fifteen boys and fifteen girls experienced five value clarification activities. The study observed positive change in the structure of the value system of adolescents. The experience level of the facilitator and the sex of students were important variables in influencing the change.

Makenzie (1980) studied the effect of value clarification interventions with moral dilemmas on moral reasoning of high school children. No change was found in moral reasoning in case of substantial majority of students.

Patric (1980) conducted an experiment to investigate the effectiveness of value clarification activities on the terminal and instrumental values of eighth grade students. The students were randomly assigned to two experimental groups and two control groups. The findings indicated that experimental groups differed significantly from the control group. The study concluded that value clarification approach was useful to students in clarifying their terminal and instrumental values.

Singh and Singh (1989) conducted an experiment entitled "Effectiveness of value clarifying strategies in Value Orientation of B.Ed. students". The sample comprised of 113 students from four different colleges in four different cities. The experimental group had 50 students while the control group had 63 students. Five values — co-operation, dedication to teaching profession, nationalism, scientific outlook and perseverence — were assessed using the Value Orientation Test Battery. It was found that the value clarification approach group was significantly superior compared to the conventional method group with respect to dedication, co-operation, nationalism and scientific outlook.

Singh (1988) conducted an experimental study on "Comparison of Value Discussion Model with Conventional Approach in Terms of Value Clarification of B.Ed. students". The sample consisted of 40 female B.Ed. student-teachers divided equally between control and experimental groups. The study adopted multiple quasi-experimental design and used Value Orientation Test Battery to assess value orientation. Values assessed under the study were co-operation, dedication to teaching profession, nationalism, scientific outlook and perseverence. The Value Discussion Model was found effective in terms of dedication to teaching profession and perseverence when measured immediately at the end of the treatment when both the groups were matched with respect to intelligence.

Singh (1991) studied comparative effectiveness of Value Discussion Model with traditional approach for developing value clarification of college students. The experiment was conducted at two stages — tryout and field. At the tryout stage the sample consisted of 233 college-going men and women while at field stage the sample size was 127 — 63 for the experimental group and 64 for the control group. Dilemmas and discussion were the major components of the model used as a treatment. Data were collected by using Value Clarification Test and Value Judgement Test. Results showed that Value Discussion Model was effective in developing Value Clarification ability of the students and the change in Value Judgement of students treated with Value Discussion Model was significant.

King (1995) conducted a study entitled "Teaching for Thinking and Citizenship Education : Examining the Constitution of Student-citizens in Secondary Social Studies".

Informed by post-structural and critical educational theory, King's dissertation examines the emphasis given to the teaching of thinking and its association with a socially transformative citizenship in twelve Social Studies classes in four U.S. Secondary Schools. The focus of transformative citizenship is a concern for reconstructing society by developing a critical understanding of and engagement with social issues and institutions. Orienting this understanding and engagement are concerns for overcoming relations of domination and promoting a more just and equitable distribution of society's needs.

The study revealed that for many teachers teaching for thinking and citizenship primarily involved the transmission of knowledge. Even teachers who embraced a multicultural perspective tended to equate it with simply adding content about diverse, under-represented groups to an already inflated curriculum.

The most thoughtful treatment of civic related content, however, was more closely associated with a socially progressive commitment on part of students and this commitment cut across gender and racial or ethnic lines.

The two trends evident in these classes — critiquing conditions of racial oppressions and connecting personally relevant concerns of students to public issues, appeared to have altered the regulative discourse of the classroom, thereby opening up possibilities for a more transformative citizenship.

Caspi (1994) conducted a study on a group of sixth grade children reading selected short stories and novels with female main characters. Literature discussion groups and written journals were used to facilitate response. The study incorporated both qualitative and quantitative methodologies. 'The Attitudes towards Women's scale for adolescents and a questionnaire in Likert scale format were used as pre- and post-measures. Other tools were the Brook's Occupational Survey, Revised and Flood and Lapp's coding system for analyzing literary discussion.

Significant progress was observed in the discussion groups and the students became more engaged in literature.

Achieving Sex Equity Through Students (ASETS) was the focus of the experiment conducted by Cote-Bonanno (1994). The study examined attitudes of High School students (110 in control group and 91 in experimental group) towards women in non-traditional occupations and on their sex-role concept. Gender, age and mother's employment status were also examined. Findings of the study suggest that ASETS made good impact on the students. Girls were more accepting of women non-traditional occupations and ASETS trained 15-year old students were more accepting than the control group. Fourteen and eighteen years old boys and girls in experimental group were found to be more androgynous in sex role concept than the control group.

From the review of literature it is seen that value-education/ value-development studies have not paid attention to gender-equality as a value. Also, programmes on gender-sensitization are on increase in India, but no systematic research as yet has been taken up to evaluate the impact of these programmes and effectiveness of various communication strategies adopted in these programmes.

3

METHODOLOGY

The present chapter discusses in detail the methodology of the study which includes design of the study, sample for data collection and the sampling procedure used, description of the research tools and techniques of data collection, and procedure adopted for developing and pretesting the tools. The chapter also elaborates on the organization of data collection, administration of the treatment, i.e. the Value Discussion Model and the scheme of analysis for quantitative and qualitative data.

DESIGN OF THE STUDY

A Quasi-experimental approach with pretest-pasttest non-equivalent group design was adopted for the study.. As explained by Tuckman (1972) "Quasi-experimental designs exist for situations in which complete experimental control is difficult or impossible". School systems often may not allow intact classes to be disrupted or divided to provide for random or equivalent samples and there are limitations in manipulating conditions. Quasi-experimental designs carry experimental control to its reasonable limit within the realities of a particular situation.

The pretest-posttest non-equivalent group design suggested by Campbell and Stanley (1963) is symbolised as :

$O_1 X O_2$ where O_1, O_3 = Pretests
X = Treatment
O_3 C O_4 O_2, O_4 = Posttests
C = Control

The study was conducted with two groups of students — one designated as the experimental group and the other as the control group. The groups were taken as they existed and were assigned the treatment randomly.

SAMPLE AND SAMPLING PROCEDURE

The study focused on adolescents and the effect of Value Discussion as treatment was to be evaluated with reference to adolescents. The content of the treatment was found more appropriate for students in the age group of 15 to 17 years. Students in the Standards 10, 11 and 12 normally fall under this age group. Students of Standard 10 and 12 have to appear for the State Board examinations, the results of which are crucial from the point of view of further studies. Hence the students of Standards 10 and 12 as well as the school authorities were reluctant about their participation in the study. Similarly, there was also reluctance in allowing students from the Science stream to participate because of more weightage given to academic achievement and timely completion of the syllabus.

Students of Standard 11 belonging to the General stream were, therefore, selected as the population for the study.

Two classes of Standard 11 of General stream were selected for the study from two schools of Vadodara. The two schools were matched on important characteristics to ensure that the students in control group and experimental group belonged to a comparable socio-academic milieu. Both the schools had Gujarati as the medium of instruction and followed the same curriculum and text-books. Both were co-educational and catered to students with comparable socio-economic background and academic achievement. The schools were situated in two different geographic areas at a considerable distance from each other, reducing the chances of contamination between the control group and the experimental group.

In random assignment of treatment, one school was designated as the experimental school while the other was treated as the control group, taking the groups of students in Standard 11, General stream, as they existed.

Description of the Sample

The total sample for the study was 145 adolescents studying in Standard 11 of General stream. The number of students in the Control group was 79 and that in the Experimental group 66.

Tables 3.1 and 3.2 summarise the characteristics of the Control and Experimental groups respectively on the basis of the independent variables selected for the study, namely, sex of the subject, education of mother, education of father, profession of mother, profession of father, and type of family.

The Control Group

Table 3.1 shows that the proportions of male and female students were almost equal in the Control group. Only 10.1 % of students had mothers having a diploma or graduation level of education and only 2.5 % of students had mothers with a post-graduate or professional degree. 55.7 % of students formed the majority with their mothers having completed high school education. With respect to father's education a majority of students fell in the middle two categories — High school (34.2%) and Diploma/Graduation (31.6%). There was, again, almost equal proportion of students falling in the two extreme categories: 12.7 % (0 to Std.7) and 13.6 % (Post-graduate or Professional degree).

An overwhelming majority of students (78.5%) had mothers who were housewives, whereas 16.5 % of students had mothers either self-employed or in service.

With respect to father's profession, almost 50 % of students had fathers in white-collar jobs. The remaining were divided between farming, business or trading (26.6%), professionals (8.9%) and labour (3.8%).

The proportion of students belonging to nuclear families was much greater (78.5%) than those belonging to joint families (17.7%).

The Experimental Group

The Experimental group differed slightly in sex-wise composition from the Control group. The percentage of female students was higher

TABLE 3.1: Description of the Control Group : Sample Size 79

	Male 40 (50.6%)		Female 39 (49.4%)		Total 79* (100%)	
Mother's Education						
0 - Std. 7	11	(13.9%)	09	(11.4%)	20	(25.3%)
Std.8 - SSC	20	(25.3%)	24	(30.4%)	44	(55.7%)
Diploma/Graduate	04	(05.1%)	04	(05.1%)	08	(10.1%)
Post-Graduate/ Professional degree	01	(01.3%)	01	(01.3%)	02	(02.5%)
Father's Education						
0 - Std. 7	07	(08.9%)	03	(03.8%)	10	(12.7%)
Std.8 - SSC	10	(12.7%)	17	(21.5%)	27	(34.2%)
Diploma/Graduate	12	(15.2%)	13	(16.5%)	25	(31.6%)
Post-Graduate/ Professional degree	06	(07.6%)	05	(06.3%)	11	(13.9%)
Mother's Profession						
Self-employed	03	(03.8%)	01	(01.3%)	04	(05.1%)
Service	03	(03.8%)	06	(07.6%)	09	(11.4%)
Housewife	31	(39.2%)	31	(39.2%)	62	(78.5%)
Father's Profession						
Labour	01	(01.3%)	02	(02.5%)	03	(03.8%)
Farming, business, trading etc.	13	(16.5%)	08	(10.1%)	21	(26.6%)
White-collar job	17	(21.5%)	23	(29.1%)	40	(50.6%)
Professional	03	(03.8%)	04	(05.1%)	07	(08.9%)
Type of Family						
Joint	07	(09.9%)	07	(09.9%)	14	(17.7%)
Nuclear	31	(39.2%)	31	(39.2%)	62	(78.5%)

* The grand total (%wise) for each variable may not come to 100% as some subjects may not have given information on that variable.

TABLE 3.2: Description of the Experimental Group : Sample Size 66

	Male 29 (43.9%)		Female 37 (56.1%)		Total 66* (100%)	
Mother's Education						
0 - Std. 7	04	(06.1%)	05	(07.8%)	09	(13.6%)
Std. 8 - SSC	17	(25.8%)	25	(37.9%)	42	(63.6%)
Diploma/Graduate	03	(04.5%)	05	(07.6%)	08	(12.1%)
Post-Graduate/ Professional degree	01	(01.5%)	00	(00.0%)	01	(01.5%)
Father's Education						
0 - Std. 7	01	(01.5%)	01	(01.5%)	02	(03.0%)
Std. 8 - SSC	11	(16.7%)	16	(24.2%)	27	(40.9%)
Diploma/Graduate	11	(16.7%)	11	(16.7%)	22	(33.3%)
Post-Graduate/ Professional degree	02	(03.0%)	07	(10.6%)	09	(13.6%)
Mother's Profession						
Self-employed	03	(04.5%)	01	(01.5%)	04	(06.1%)
Service	00	(00.0%)	01	(01.5%)	01	(01.5%)
Housewife	24	(36.4%)	33	(50.0%)	57	(86.4%)
Father's Profession						
Labour	01	(01.5%)	05	(07.8%)	06	(09.1%)
Farming, business, trading etc.	12	(18.2%)	11	(16.7%)	23	(34.8%)
White-collar job	08	(12.1%)	14	(21.2%)	22	(33.3%)
Professional	04	(06.1%)	05	(07.6%)	09	(13.6%)
Type of Family						
Joint	11	(16.7%)	11	(16.7%)	22	(33.3%)
Nuclear	16	(24.2%)	24	(36.4%)	40	(60.6%)

* The grand total (%wise) for each variable may not come to 100% as some subjects may not have given information on that variable.

(56.1%) than that of male students (43.9%).

Majority of students (63.6%) had mothers with high school education. Only 12.1% had mothers having a diploma or graduation level of education while only 1.5 % of students had mothers with a post-graduate or professional degree. With respect to mother's education the composition of the two groups shows a similar pattern. The Experimental group, however, has a smaller proportion of students (13.6%) having mothers whose education ended before reaching high school, compared to the Control group (25.3%).

A similar pattern is also observed in the two groups with respect to father's education. In the Experimental group 40.9 % of students had fathers who had completed high school education and 33.3 % of students had fathers with a diploma or graduate degree. 13.6% of students had fathers with a post-graduate or professional degree. But again the proportion of students having fathers whose education ended before reaching high school is smaller in the Experimental group (3.0%) compared to the Control group (12.7%).

In the Experimental group too, an overwhelming majority (86.4%) of students had mothers who were housewives while only 7.6 % of students had mothers either self-employed or in service.

In the Experimental group a large majority of students were almost equally divided between the middle two categories with respect to father's profession. 34.8% of students had fathers in farming, business or trading, while 33.3% of students had fathers in white-collar jobs. Those students having fathers in the categories of labour (9.1%) and professionals (13.6%) were slightly higher in proportion compared to the Control group.

The Experimental group also had a majority of students (60.6%) belonging to nuclear families. The proportion of students (33.3%) belonging to joint families was, however, higher compared to the Control group (17.7%).

DATA REQUIRED FOR THE STUDY

The study aimed at evaluating the effect of Value Discussion Model on adolescents in terms of change in the following dependent variables : (i) attitude towards gender equality, (ii) gender stereotypes, (iii) value judgement, and (iv) value clarification. Pretest and posttest scores of both the experimental and the control groups were required for the study.

The independent variables included in the study were sex of the subject, education of mother and father, professions of mother and father, and type of family. Data regarding these variables were required from each individual.

Mere quantitative data and statistical analysis could not reveal the subtle aspects of change in the adolescents. Besides, the treatment was spread over a span of four months and hence focusing only on pre- and post-scores would ignore happenings between the two points. Considering these points qualitative data in form of day-to-day observations and content of student discussion were included in the study.

TOOLS OF MEASUREMENT

Description of the Research Tools

The following tools developed by the investigator were used for collection of data for the study. The same versions of the tools were used for the pretests and the posttests in both the control as well as the experimental groups. (Appendices 1 to 4 show actual samples of the tools.)

Self-Administered Questionnaire

A short self-administered questionnaire entitled 'Background Information' was used to collect information about the independent variables. It required the participants to fill in appropriate information in a few words about their sex, education of mother and father, profession of mother and father, and type of family. Though there was a space for writing name, students were given freedom of not writing the name. (Appendix 1)

Attitude Scale

A Likert-type attitude scale was used to assess attitude towards gender equality. The scale had 26 attitude statements; 10 positive and 16 negative. Against each statement were given five response categories —"strongly agree, agree, undecided, disagree and strongly disagree". Following the Likert method of summated ratings, each response was given a weight in the range of 0 to 4 and a total score for each student was obtained by summating scores for all the individual items (Likert, 1932). The maximum score on the scale was 104, and the minimum score was 0. (Appendix 2)

Gender Stereotype Tests

To assess gender stereotyping, 'professions' was selected as the dimension.

The profession test was a check-list of 50 professions with three response categories against each item : (a) the profession is appropriate for men, (b) the profession is appropriate for women, (c) the profession is appropriate for both. Additionally, participants were required to give reasons in brief if they believed that a particular profession was not appropriate either for men or women. The maximum score on the test was 50 and the minimum score was 0. (Appendix 3)

Value Test

A common tool was used to evaluate the change in value judgement and value clarification of participants with reference to gender equality. The test comprised of twelve situations derived from experiences of adolescents in their day-to-day life. Under each situation four alternatives were given to participants from which they had to choose one. This part of the test gave a quantitative score (ranging from 1 to 3) to each value judgement showing 'to what extent the participant valued gender equality'. The maximum score on the test was 36 and the minimum score was 12.

The second part of the test required students to give reasons for their choice of a particular alternative which were analysed qualitatively to assess the level of normative arguments. (Appendix 4)

All the tools were prepared in Gujarati language as the medium of instruction for the control group and the experimental group was Gujarati, and the investigator has good command over the language.

Methods to Record Qualitative Data

Detailed Notes on Dilemma Sessions

The investigator maintained a detailed step-by-step record of each dilemma and discussion session which included the theme of dilemma, date, time and mode of presentation, alternatives put before participants, the pre-discussion response of students and formation of small groups on the basis of their choice, arguments presented by each group in support of their choice, the discussion that followed, probe-questions by the investigator and the discussion generated by probe-questions, and the post-discussion response by the students. (Appendix 5)

Record of Observations

From the day of the first visit to the schools to the end, a record of observations was maintained by the investigator. It included recording of students behaviour (whatever the investigator found striking or interesting from her' subjective angle) before, during and after the dilemma session; informal chats among students and with investigator during the break; teachers' comments; and also the overall atmosphere of the school.

Written Summary of Arguments presented by Participants

After presentation of each dilemma and posing of the alternatives by the investigator, the participants indicated their choice by putting the serial number of the chosen alternative on a slip of paper and passing it to the investigator. These slips helped decide the number of participants in favour of each alternative.

Small discussion groups were formed on the basis of the choice. Each group discussed among themselves, and before presenting their arguments to the class, wrote them down. The investigator collected these papers at the end of every session. They gave an idea of students' feelings about the issue in their own words.

After the discussion students voted again (this was voluntary) and the slips with the serial number of alternative chosen helped decide the post-discussion response of participants. (Appendix 6)

Construction of Tools

All the tools used for data collection were developed by the investigator as no appropriate standardised tools focusing on the same content and population were available. Two versions of each tool were prepared — an English version was prepared for some of the experts who did not know Gujarati and for later inclusion in the dissertation document, while the Gujarati version was used for data collection.

The investigator followed a step-by-step approach for constructing the tools. The process began with reviewing theoretical literature on constructs to be measured, viz. attitudes, stereotypes and values. Literature on construction of attitude scales, check-lists and various other types of tools was also referred and later examples of similar tools were reviewed from research reports. Expert evaluation and field testing were carried out before preparing the final versions of the tools.

(i) Construction of Attitude Scale

Attitude is the degree of positive or negative affect associated with some psychological object. A psychological object is any symbol, phrase, slogan, person, institution, ideal or idea towards which people can differ with respect to positive or negative affect.

The concept of attitude is a broad one. Attitude theorists have proposed that there are separable components of the attitude concept. These components are classified as Cognitive, Affective and Conative. The cognitive component of an attitude includes the beliefs, the perceptions and the information one has about the attitude object. It is fact-oriented but it cannot be separated from evaluation. The affective component of an attitude refers to the emotional feelings about or the liking or disliking of the attitude object. The conative component refers to one's policy orientation towards the attitude object or one's stance about the way in which persons (or attitude objects) should be treated in specific social contexts (Wrightsman, 1977).

Edwards (1969) has summarised the suggestions given by Wang, Thurstone and Chave, Likert, Bird, and Edwards and Kilpatrick for construction of attitude scales. With the help of these guidelines a Likert-type attitude-scale was constructed by the investigator to assess the change in attitude towards gender equality due to the treatment.

Attitude statements were prepared based on various dimensions of gender equality, e.g. personal consequences for men and women, social and national consequences, desirability, and support to the movement for equality. Statements were selected in such a way that cognitive, affective and conative components were represented with reference to attitude towards gender equality. These statements were edited using the criteria suggested by Edwards (1969).

35 statements were included in the first draft of the attitude scale. These items were scrutinised by the evaluation experts to ensure that each item was an 'attitude statement' (i.e. people can differ on it with respect to positive or negative affect). The items were also passed by experts on gender studies as reflecting an aspect related to gender equality.

Item Analysis

Item analysis using statistical method was done for the attitude scale on a sample of 90 adolescent boys and girls. As suggested by Edwards (1969), the frequency distribution of scores was considered, based upon the responses to all the statements. 25 subjects with the highest scores and 25 subjects with the lowest scores were then identified and *t*-test was applied for evaluating the response of the high and low groups to the individual statements. The value of '*t*' gave the measure of the extent to which a given statement differentiated between the high and low groups.

$$t = \frac{\overline{X}_H - \overline{X}_L}{\sqrt{\frac{S^2_H}{n_H} + \frac{S^2_L}{n_L}}}$$

where $\overline{X}_H$ = the mean score on a given statement for the high group.

$\overline{X}_L$ = the mean score on a given statement for the low group.

S^2_H = the variance of the distribution of responses of high group to the statement.

S^2_L = the variance of the distribution of responses of low group to the statement.

n_H = the number of subjects in the high group.

n_L = the number of subjects in the low group.

Statements having a '*t*' value greater than 1.75 showed significant difference between the two groups and hence were retained in the final draft. Out of 35 statements subjected to item analysis, 26 statements (10 positive, 16 negative) were included in the second draft of the attitude scale which was to be field-tested before the experiment.

Scoring Procedure

Against each attitude statement in the scale were given five response categories — strongly agree, agree, undecided, disagree, strongly disagree.

The scoring for individual statements was carried out as follows:

Response Category	Positive Statement	Negative Statement
Strongly agree	4	0
Agree	3	1
Undecided	2	2
Disagree	1	3
Strongly disagree	0	4

A total score (out of maximum 104) was obtained for each participant by summating scores for all the individual items.

(ii) Construction of Gender Stereotype Test

The Chambers Twentieth Century Dictionary (Chambers, 1972) defines *stereotype* as 'a fixed conventionalised representation'. Wrightsman (1977) has defined *stereotype* as a relatively rigid and oversimplified conception of a group of people, in which all individuals in the group are labelled with the so-called group characteristics. Gender stereotypes are stereotypes associated with being a man or a woman. Gender stereotypes encompass a whole range of aspects like looks, personality, behaviour, choice of profession, qualities, social roles, duties, expectations, life-style and life-goals. Reporting on several researches focusing on gender stereotypes, Wrightsman (1977) summarises : "At least two points are clear from the research on sex-role stereotypes : first, the stereotypes are pervasive and exist among a wide variety of populations — clinicians, college students, older adults and children. Second, these stereotypes are held by men and women alike, suggesting that they are a cultural rather than a male chauvinist phenomenon."

Professions were selected as the dimension for the test because they fall in the purview of immediate observations and experiences of the adolescents.

A person's profession plays an important role in determining his or her social status. Apart from demanding same pay for same work and equal opportunity for promotion, advocates of equality argue that both women and men should be given the opportunity to pursue any of the jobs that society has to offer. In reality, however, people label certain jobs as 'male jobs' and certain others as 'female jobs'. Sometimes these labels are based on social observations. For example, one has seen very few male pre-school teachers or female pilots. At times, some jobs are seen as the 'natural' extension of women's traditional roles (for example, job of a baby sitter), and hence are labelled as female jobs. People apply several other criteria like physical strength, the type of skill required, work hours, the job-related need to travel or stay away from home, pay and prestige associated with the job based on their unconscious assumptions about gender roles, in labelling jobs as 'male' or 'female'. Rapid development in contraception and modern technology has, however, brought a tremendous change in the work arena. Educated women now spend very few years in child bearing and new technology has opened many jobs to women, jobs which earlier required physical strength. And yet, gender stereotyping in profession is very much alive.

For constructing the profession test to assess stereotyping among participants, a list of seventy different professions was compiled. The list included a wide range including conventionally male and conventionally female professions, professions with higher and lower social respectability and different levels of income.

The list was then given to five adolescents of Standard 11 from a school which catered to students of comparable socio-economic and academic achievement levels. These adolescents studied the list and marked the professions which were totally unfamiliar to them. Ten such professions were then taken out from the test. A list of remaining sixty professions was then given for scrutiny to three experts who had worked in the area of evaluation, gender studies and vocational guidance. These experts had to finalise the list of professions considered conventionally male or conventionally female, but which could actually be taken up by both, men and women. The experts also advised to include a few professions which were more or less considered androgynous.

A final list of 50 professions was drawn up which reflected a wide spectrum of skills, income and respectability levels and fields.

Scoring Procedure

Against each profession spaces were specified for marking the response:

Profession	Appropriate for Men	Appropriate for Women	Reason

If the respondent felt that the profession was appropriate for both, men and women, he or she had to mark in both the boxes. Each respondent was given three scores : *M, F* and *T* where the '*M*' score indicated the number of professions designated as 'appropriate only for men', the '*F*' score indicated the number of professions designated as 'appropriate only for women' and the '*T*' score indicated the number of professions designated as 'appropriate for men and women' — higher the '*T*' score, lower the level of gender stereotyping with respect to professions. The maximum possible '*T*' score was 50.

The respondents were asked to give a reason when they marked a profession appropriate only for men or only for women. These reasons were coded in eight different categories (for details please refer to Chapter 4 — Analysis of Data).

(iii) Construction of Value Test

A common tool was constructed to assess the change in value judgement and value clarification with reference to gender equality.

According to Shaver and Williams (1976), Value Judgements are the assertions we make on the basis of our values. In order to make a Value Judgement one considers all facts in a situation, thinks of possible consequences of each alternative, and on the basis of some criteria developed by the individual, decides which alternative action one would take. The criteria indicate what one prizes most and what one values (Das, 1987). According to Rowntree (1981), Value Judgement is a person's subjective appraisal of quality or worth of someone or something based on his own value system or that of his peers. According to Hersh (1980), Value Judging requires the ability to evaluate conflicting interests in the light of a consistent criterion or principle.

Review of literature on Value Clarification indicates wide acceptance of Raths (1966)'s concept of value clarification wherein seven valuing processes are given as components of value clarification. They are (i) choosing freely, (ii) choosing from alternatives, (iii) choosing after considering the consequences, (iv) prizing and cherishing, (v) publicly affirming, (vi) acting upon choices, and (vii) repeating.

For constructing the value test, situations from day-to-day life of adolescents were developed which required the respondents to give a value judgement based on their value of gender equality. Each situation included one or more of the value clarification processes proposed by Raths (1966). Under each situation four alternatives were given. The first three alternatives showed different levels of valuing gender equality while the fourth was an open-ended alternative allowing students to advance an option other than the three given options. Respondents had to choose one of the alternatives.

After developing sixteen such situations and writing the first draft of the test, it was given to a panel of five experts and three school teachers to scrutinise the situations and alternatives given. Three experts and all the teachers suggested that since the test also required the respondents to give reasons for their choice, sixteen situations would be too many for the students to attempt. It was hence decided to cut down the number of situations to twelve. The situations involved personal action, interpersonal or public advocacy, protesting against bias in family, school or in public, or open acceptance of one's value for gender equality.

The second part of the response required respondents to give reasons for their choice of a particular alternative. According to Facione *et al.* (1978), an important step towards understanding what people mean by their normative claims is to ask for reasons why we should accept their normative views.

Facione *et al.* (1978) have also suggested a procedure for assessing normative arguments, which focuses upon distinguishing between 'justifications' and 'pseudo-justifications'. "Justifications are reasons that would persuade unbiased, informed, rational people that our normative positions are, beyond any reasonable doubt, correct."

By analysing the reasons given for supporting the value judgement one can distinguish pseudo-justifications based on the following criteria :

(i) Giving one's motivations is not justification. "I would do it because I enjoy it", or "I would not choose it because it scares me". These are personal motivations which should not be confused with justification.

(ii) Appeals to emotion aimed at directly bringing about action do not constitute justification.

(iii) Rationalization is not justification. To rationalise is to choose first and look for the reason later.

(iv) Excuses are not justifications.

(v) Citation of facts about the sources of the views that are being defended is not equivalent to citation of reasons. For example, endorsement of parents, scripture, authority, custom or public opinion is not a sufficient basis for justification.

If facts provided in support are false, irrelevant or inconclusive, then they fail to be basis for justification.

For assessment of the level of normative arguments Piaget's stages of distributive justice also give some guidelines. At Stage-1 the subjects consider that whatever the authority says is the law. At Stage-2 designated as egalitarianism rigid equality is proposed whatever the situation, whereas at Stage-3 called equity, equality is always defined taking into account the way each individual is situated (Wrightsman, 1977).

The qualitative analysis of the reasons given in the twelve situations on the value test has been done in the light of the theoretical basis of value clarification discussed above.

Establishing Validity and Reliability of the Tools

The validity of a test, or of any measuring tool, depends upon the fidelity with which it measures what it purports to measure. Validity is a relative term. A test is valid for a particular purpose or in a particular situation — it is not generally valid (Garrett and

Woodsworth, 1961). The content validity involves essentially a systematic examination of test content to determine whether it covers a representative sample of the behaviour to be measured.

Content validity of all the four tools was established by submitting them to a thorough scrutiny by a panel of five experts. The experts belonged to the fields of Education and Psychology, Gender Studies, and Human Development and Family Studies.

In addition, five school teachers normally teaching in the Class 11 were asked to evaluate the tests for clarity of language and meaning; and structure of the test with respect to ease of answering.

The scoring procedure for all the four tools were also approved by three experts in evaluation and measurement.

According to Garrett and Woodsworth (1961) a test score is called reliable when we have reasons for believing the score to be stable and trustworthy. Reliability of tools was determined through test-retest method. The test-retest reliability refers to consistency of scores obtained by the same individual when re-examined with the same test on a different occasion. The test-retest procedure was carried out in the class of Standard 11 of Navyug School. The common sample size for the test and the retest was 80 boys and girls and the time-gap between the test and the retest was of 30 days. The correlation coefficient was worked out on the basis of the scores obtained by 80 students on the test and the retest. The correlation coefficient was found to be 0.79 for the attitude scale and 0.77 for the gender stereotype test.

Field-Testing of Tools

All the tools were field tested in April 1993 in the same school which later was to become the experimental school. A sample size of 90 boys and girls was selected at random from two classes of Standard 11. The actual experiment was scheduled to begin in the next academic term (in July-August 1993). At that time the students on whom field testing was done moved to Standard 12 which was not part of the experiment. This reduced their chances of reappearing on the same test to a minimum. (Only a student failing in Standard 11 in the examination of May 1993 had a chance of reappearance but none of the students in the sample failed.)

Besides giving response to the items in the test, the respondents had to underline words and statements difficult to understand; state whether the instructions were clear and format convenient to respond, and opine whether attempting the test was interesting or boring.

For each test, the time taken for the first student and the last student to complete the test were also noted to see if the tests could be completed by a majority of students in a reasonable time. Students were also asked to comment freely on whether they would like to participate in such a programme.

After field-testing the following modifications were made : mother's and father's education were added as variables, clear-cut boxes were introduced as space for marking responses, difficult words were deleted, changed or explained using brackets, and certain instructions were made clear. Students' comments showed that they treated the programme as useful and a welcome change in which they could freely discuss their ideas.

ORGANIZATION OF DATA COLLECTION

The data collection was organised in the following phases: conducting the pretests, administering the treatment and conducting the posttests. Qualitative data collection was carried out throughout the period of the experiment.

Conducting the Pretests

The two groups selected as sample were randomly assigned to experimental and control status. Both the groups were given the pretests using the same tools developed by the investigator for the present study. For each group the pretesting lasted two days. On the day one the groups responded to the self-administered questionnaire for background information and the attitude scale, while on the second day they were given the gender stereotype test and the value test.

Administering the Treatment

After the pretests, the control group students continued to engage in the activities they normally did while the experimental group, in addition to their normal activities, participated in the treatment sessions.

Out of several strategies and models concerned with value clarification, moral education and communication, the Value Discussion Model developed by Sansanwal in 1986 was chosen as the treatment because it was the only model developed and validated in India, was comparatively recent and its approach was found to be consistent with the philosophy and paradigm of the Development Support Communication. It was also found suitable for the sample (Adolescents) and the content (Gender Equality). (Please refer to Conceptual Framework in Chapter 1 for details.)

Components of Value Discussion Model

Dilemma and Discussion are the two main components of Value Discussion Model.

Dilemmas are stories which present a central character in a problematic situation for which there are several possible responses and in which number of issues come in conflict. Dilemma should present a problematic situation to which there is no single obvious right answer. An effective dilemma must offer a choice of actions and pose the question : "What should the central character do?"

The success of the model to a large extent depends on the way discussion is held. The students must feel free to give their opinions and share feelings. They should not feel censured or embarrassed and their views are not to be evaluated. The researcher's role is to present the dilemma, encourage free discussion and intervene only when the flow of discussion goes off-track or gets stuck. Listening to adolescents in their own language, identifying their concerns and thinking process was also important for the present research.

Selection of Content and Developing the Dilemmas

The content selection for the experiment was done after extensive reading on gender equality issues (books, journals, research and committee reports, official documents and activist/grassroots publications) as well as from other communication media like television, films and radio.

The following criteria were considered for selection of content: age appropriateness, familiarity to the group, relevance to the group; scope for generating value conflict and providing opportunity for analysis, synthesis, evaluation, rethinking, questioning and decision making; and encompassing various aspects of gender issues — home and family, work and economic sphere, law, social norms and moral standards, education, politics, public life and policy planning.

Sixty dilemmas were developed to begin with. They were discussed with a group of five adolescents in the neighbourhood, two secondary school teachers, two experts from the Department of Human Development and Family Studies and a group of five students of the class of Post-Graduate Degree in Journalism and Communication of the Maharaja Sayajirao University of Baroda. As a result of these discussion sessions twenty dilemmas getting the highest preference were identified for inclusion in the treatment.

Presenting the Dilemmas

Dilemmas were presented to students in Gujarati at the rate of one dilemma a day. The following communication modes and media were used for presenting the dilemmas in an interesting and effective way :

— video recordings
— audio recordings
— film clips
— television snippets
— advertisements
— newspaper clippings
— oral and written presentations with the help of a blackboard
— role-play
— puppets

Detailed outlines of dilemmas with modes of presentation are given in Appendix 6.

Organizing Small Group Discussion

Once a dilemma was presented each student took a tentative position about what action the central character should take. A good dilemma usually generates a division within the class on the action the central character should take.

Small group discussion maximised student-to-student interaction and generated thinking about reasons for supporting a particular position. Students felt more comfortable in small groups because all members of a single group had made the same decision and they got an opportunity to contribute to the discussion with relatively lower risk of failure or resistance.

Students were allowed to switch from one group to another if in the midst of the discussion they decided to change their position on action.

While students met in small groups, the investigator moved from one group to another helping students focus on the position taken by them, clarify their reasoning and list the best reasons for the position taken by the group.

Conducting the Class Discussion

The class discussion gave students an opportunity to report the reasoning which supported their position, to hear other reasons given for the same position and to hear reasons for other positions. They challenged reasoning of other groups and at the same time their own reasoning got challenged. As students debated the merits of one reason over another, they engaged in mental activities that facilitated value clarification and judgement.

In the class discussion the investigator had two main tasks : to promote interaction among students and to keep the discussion focused on the value. The investigator used probe questions to help students examine issues they had ignored or to think of proper justifications in place of pseudo-justifications, to think about reasoning at a higher stage.

Probe questions would facilitate Value Clarification process because they help students :

— to think increasingly in more generalizable terms,
— to develop an increasingly broad societal perspective,
— to focus increasingly on the larger value issues implicit in a dilemma.

Appendix 5 gives detailed description of the Proceedings of entire Value Discussion Session.

Closing the Discussion

Students with the help of the investigator, summarised on the blackboard all the reasons given for the choice of different positions. Thereafter the students had to individually choose the position which finally appealed to them, put it on a piece of paper and pass it to the investigator.

Public declaration of the positions taken by students was encouraged but there was no pressure for it, nor was there any direct or indirect pressure for a particular choice. The investigator refrained from passing judgement or evaluating the choices made by the students.

Running notes and a detailed diary was meticulously maintained by the investigator recording every dilemma discussion session. Appendix 6 gives for pre-discussion and post-discussion choices given by students for each dilemma.

Out of the 20 dilemmas selected for the experiment, only 16 dilemmas could be discussed in four months. Problems were many, interruptions frequent. Often sessions had to be cancelled at the last minute following electricity failure or sudden death of a student or of a political leader. Holidays were many. School cricket matches found half the students missing from the class. A strike to oppose hike in the bus-fare paralysed work for fifteen days and examinations meant that students were not available first due to study leave, then due to actual examination and a couple of days after that they remained in celebration mood.

Conducting the Posttests

One week after the completion of Value Discussion Sessions in the experimental group, posttests were conducted in both the groups. The same tools that were used for the pretests were used for the posttests. For each group the posttesting lasted for two days. On the first day the groups responded to the attitude scale and the profession test while on the second day they were given the value test.

Preparation for Data Analysis

Each respondent in the control group and the experimental group was given a numerical code for identification and scoring was done for each test according to the scoring procedure already discussed in detail.

The independent variables were categorised and given numerical codes. For example, mother's education and father's education were classified in four categories :

Code	*Category*
4	Professional degree or post-graduation
3	Diploma, graduation, some college education

Code	*Category*
2	Standard 8 to S.S.C.
1	0 to Standard 7

Codes were also given to reasons in the profession test. Computerised data entry was used for greater ease, speed and scope for analysis and the data were analysed with the help of Statistical Package for Social Sciences (SPSS). The statistical techniques were decided after consulting a statistician with experience in educational and social science research. Frequencies, percentages, *t*-test and ANCOVA were used to test various hypotheses. The details and results of analysis are presented in Chapter 4.

4

ANALYSIS OF DATA

The present chapter discusses in detail different techniques used for analysis of quantitative and qualitative data and the outcome of the analysis.

CHANGE IN ATTITUDE TOWARDS GENDER EQUALITY

Comparison of Adjusted Mean Attitude towards Gender Equality of Experimental Group and of Control Group

Adjusted mean attitude towards gender equality of experimental group was compared with the control group by considering the pretest scores of the same variable as co-variate. The data were analysed using ANCOVA and the results of analysis are presented in Table 4.1.

TABLE 4.1 : Summary of ANCOVA for Attitude towards Gender Equality taking Treatment as a Source of Variance

Source of Variance	df	SSy.x	MSSy.x	Fy.x
Treatment	1	209.260	209.260	0.283
Error	94	69624.889	740.690	

Table 4.1 shows that the adjusted F-value is 0.283 which is not significant at 0.05 level. It can, therefore, be concluded that the treatment had no significant effect on change of attitude towards gender equality.

To find out if the Value Discussion Model as treatment was effective in changing the attitude of the students towards gender equality, in the experimental group the null hypothesis (no. 4) was tested with the help of paired samples *t*-test/correlational *t*-test. Table

4.2 shows the sample means and SE of pretest and posttest scores and the t-value for the control and the experimental groups.

TABLE 4.2 : Testwise Mean, SE and 't' value of Attitude towards Gender Equality in the Control Group and the Experimental Group

Control Group					Experimental Group				
Test	Mean	SE	r	t-value	Test	Mean	SE	r	t-value
Pre-Test	75.82	2.83	0.75	0.31	Pre-Test	81.14	1.84	0.36	1.76
Post-Test	76.48	3.19			Post-Test	84.86	1.91		

From Table 4.2 it can be seen that for the control group the correlated t-value is 0.31 which is not significant at 0.05 level. For the experimental group the correlated t-value is 1.76 which is also not significant at 0.05 level. It indicates that the treatment of Value Discussion Model did not significantly affect attitude towards gender equality.

CHANGE IN GENDER STEREOTYPING

Comparison of Adjusted Mean Gender-Stereotyping by Experimental Group and by Control Group

Adjusted mean gender-stereotyping by the experimental group and by the control group were compared by considering the pretest scores on the same variable as co-variate. The results of the ANCOVA are summarised in Table 4.3.

TABLE 4.3 : Summary of ANCOVA for Gender-Stereotyping taking Treatment as a Source of Variance

Source of Variance	df	SSy.x	MSSy.x	Fy.x
Treatment	1	962.939	962.939	22.68**
Error	61	2589.909	42.458	

** Significant at 0.01 level.

It can be seen from Table 4.3 that the adjusted F-value is 22.68 which is significant at 0.05 as well as 0.01 levels. This indicates that the effect of treatment on the two groups, with respect to gender-stereotyping differed significantly.

To find out if the Value Discussion Model as treatment was effective in changing gender stereotyping in the experimental group the null hypothesis (no. 5) was tested with the help of paired samples t-test/correlated t-test.

TABLE 4.4 : Testwise Mean, SE and 't' Value of Gender-Stereotyping (*vis-a-vis* Professions) in the Control Group and the Experimental Group

Control Group					Experimental Group				
Test	Mean	SE	r	t-value	Test	Mean	SE	r	t-value
Pre-Test	31.68	1.60			Pre-Test	37.33	0.79		
			0.70	1.00				0.05	4.08**
Post-Test	30.36	1.78			Post-Test	41.40	0.65		

** Significant at 0.01 level.

Table 4.4 shows that the correlated t-value for the control group is 1.00 which is not significant at 0.05 level.

The correlated t-value for the experimental group is 4.08 which is significant at 0.01 level. Hence, it may be said that Value Discussion Model as treatment significantly affected the gender-stereotyping with respect to professions. The mean pretest scores and mean posttest scores of the experimental group also reveal that the change occurred in the positive direction because the extent of gender non-stereotyping increased.

Correlated t-tests were carried out for the experimental group to further understand the change in gender-stereotyping with respect to professions labelled as 'appropriate only for women' and 'appropriate only for men'. Tables 4.5 and 4.6 present the outcome of the analysis.

Table 4.5 shows that the correlated t-value is 3.66 which is significant at 0.01 level. The mean pretest and posttest scores show that the mean posttest score is lower than the mean pretest score for professions labelled as 'appropriate only for women'. Hence it may be said that in the experimental group, Value Discussion Model was effective in bringing down gender-stereotyping with respect to professions labelled as 'appropriate only for women'.

TABLE 4.5: Testwise Mean, SE and 't' Value of Gender-Stereotyping in the Experimental Group with respect to Professions Labelled as 'Appropriate Only for Women'

Test	Mean	SE	r	t-value
Pretest	4.67	0.277	0.105	3.66**
Posttest	3.10	0.357		

** Significant at 0.01 level.

Table 4.6 shows that the correlated t-value is 2.60 which is significant at 0.05 level. The mean pretest and posttest scores show that the mean posttest score is lower than the mean pretest score for professions labelled as 'appropriate only for men'. Hence it may be said that in the experimental group, Value Discussion Model was effective in bringing down gender-stereotyping with respect to professions lebelled as 'appropriate only for men'.

TABLE 4.6 : Testwise Mean, SE and 't' Value of Gender-Stereotyping in the Experimental Group with respect to Professions labelled as 'Appropriate only for Men'

Test	Mean	SE	r	t-value
Pretest	7.67	0.640	0.001	2.60**
Posttest	5.43	0.573		

** Significant at 0.01 level.

The change in gender stereotypes with respect to professions was further analysed with the help of frequencies and percentage of *T*, *F* and *M* scores :

T	=	Profession is appropriate for both, men and women;	Higher the *T* score, lower the level of gender-stereotyping.
F	=	Profession is appropriate only for women; and	Higher the *M* and *F* score, higher the level of gender-stereotyping.
M	=	Profession is appropriate only for men.	

The frequencies and percentages of each type of score on pretests and posttests were compared to reveal more information on change with respect to each profession. This analysis was carried out for the experimental group only. Several questions were raised to gain more insight. These were :

Which professions were considered appropriate for both, men and women, by students even before they participated in the Value Discussion sessions?

Which professions were considered predominantly 'male' or predominantly 'female' and in which of these change was observed after the treatment?

Which were the professions in which no change was observed after the treatment?

The responses of students were categorized on the basis of the above questions and the following criteria based on the pretest scores were used for categorization of professions :

(i) When the *T* score (which is actually an indication of gender-non-stereotyping) on any profession is above 80% (i.e. more than 80% of students considered the profession appropriate for both genders) the profession was categorized as 'Appropriate for both, men and women'.

(ii) When the *T* score on any profession was 60% to 80% and the scores for both *F* and *M* less than 20% but the inclination towards any one gender (shown by *F* or *M* score) was more than the other, the profession was categorized as 'Appropriate for both genders but with a slight inclination towards men or women', as the case may be.

(iii) When the *T* score on any profession was 60 % to 80 % and the percentage of students inclining towards any one gender for a given profession was at least 20 % (shown by *F* or *M* scores on a profession), the profession was categorized as 'more appropriate for women' or 'more appropriate for men'.

(iv) When the percentage of students inclining towards any one gender on a given profession was higher than the percentage of students considering the profession appropriate for both genders, the profession was categorized as 'predominantly masculine' or 'predominantly feminine'.

For evaluating the change in gender-stereotyping about a

particular profession the following criteria were observed :

(i) When after the treatment the *T* score went up by more than 20 per cent on a given profession (showing reduction in gender-stereotyping and increase in non-stereotyping) and there was a reduction in *F* and *M* scores the change was considered 'Noteworthy'.

(ii) When after the treatment the *T* score went up by more than 5 % and upto 20 % the change was considered 'up to some extent'.

(iii) When after the treatment the *T* score went up by 5 % or less, the change was considered 'negligible'.

The results of the analysis are presented in the tabular summary (Tables 4.7 to 4.13) that follows:

TABLE 4.7 : Professions considered Appropriate for both, Men and Women

Professions included in the Category	Change after Treatment		
before Treatment	Noteworthy	Upto Some Extent	Negligible
Doctor			Doctor
Lawyer			Lawyer
Accountant			Accountant
Musician			Musician
Computer Engineer			Computer Engineer
Librarian			Librarian
Telephone Operator			Telephone Operator
Journalist			Journalist
Scientist			Scientist
Mathematician			Mathematician
Linguist			Linguist
Sports-person			Sports-person
Sales person			Sales person

Table 4.7 shows a list of professions considered appropriate for both genders. Even before the treatment gender-stereotyping was not observed in all these professions and after the treatment also they remained in the same category.

TABLE 4.8 : Professions considered Appropriate for both Genders but with a Slight Inclination towards Women

Professions included in the Category before Treatment	Change after Treatment		
	Noteworthy	Upto Some Extent	Negligible
Dancer		Social Worker	Dancer
Typist			Typist
Social Worker			

Table 4.8 shows that before the treatment a majority of students (more than 60%) considered the professions of dancer, typist and social worker appropriate for both genders. There were, however, some students (6% in case of typist and social worker and 14.6% in case of dancer) who considered these professions appropriate only for women. After the treatment Dancer and Typist remained in the same category whereas the *T* score for Social Worker went up from 77% to 83.6% and the *F* score came down from 6 % to 0%. The *M* score was 0 on pretest as well as posttest. Thus after the treatment the profession of Social Worker moved in the category 'appropriate for both, men and women'.

TABLE 4.9: Professions considered Appropriate for both Genders but with a Slight Inclination towards Men

Professions included in the Category before Treatment	Change after Treatment		
	Noteworthy	Upto Some Extent	Negligible
Announcer		*Announcer	Bank-teller
Computer Programmer		Computer Programmer	Police Officer
Bank-teller		*Ad Executive	Minister
Ad Executive		*Corporate Officer	Photographer
Corporate Officer		*Film Director	
Police Officer		Politician	
Film Director		*Film Producer	
Minister		Finance and Tax Consultant	
Politician		Acting	
Film Producer			
Photographer			
Finance and Tax-Consultant			
Acting			

Before the treatment there were 13 professions (listed in Table 4.9) which were considered appropriate for both genders by a majority (more than 60%) of students. There were, however, some students (ranging from 8% to 17%) who considered these professions appropriate only for men. Out of these 13 professions, negligible change was observed with regard to the professions of Bank-teller, Police officer, Minister and Photographer. They continued to remain in the same category. For the rest of the nine professions the *T* score went up by more than 5 per cent and up to 19 per cent and the *M* score came down. Despite the change, the professions of Computer programmer, Politician, Finance & Tax consultant and Actor remained in the same category as their *T* score did not rise above 80%. Five professions starred in the Table 4.9, however, moved to the category 'appropriate for both men and women' because their *T* score rose above 80%. These professions were :

Announcer	(*T* score rose from 77.6% on pretest to 83.6% on posttest and *M* score came down from 7.2% to 0);
Ad Executive	(*T* score rose from 77.6% on pretest to 83.6% on posttest and *M* score came down from 7.2% to 1.5%);
Corporate Officer	(*T* score rose from 77.6% on pretest to 83.6% on posttest and *M* score came down from 7.2% to 0);
Film Director	(*T* score rose from 72.8% on pretest to 80.6% on posttest and *M* score came down from 12.16% to 3.00%);
Film Producer	(*T* score rose from 67.64% on pretest to 80.1% on posttest and *M* score came down from 14.56% to 3.00%).

Table 4.10 shows two professions which were considered 'more appropriate for women' before the treatment. 43.28 per cent students considered the profession of Fashion Model appropriate only for women while 40.28% considered it 'appropriate for both genders'. 2.4% students considered it 'appropriate only for men'. After the treatment the percentage of students considering Fashion

Modelling appropriate for both genders (*T* score) rose from 43.28% to 61.2% and the *F* score came down from 40.28% to 17.9%. The *M* score went up from 2.4% to 7.2%. Thus, after the treatment the profession of Fashion Model moved to category 'appropriate for both genders with slight inclination towards women'.

TABLE 4.10 : Professions considered More Appropriate for Women

Professions included in the Category before Treatment	Change after Treatment		
	Noteworthy	Upto Some Extent	Negligible
Fashion Model	Fashion Model		
Dress Designer	Dress Designer		

The profession of Dress Designer was considered 'appropriate only for women' by 36.32% before the treatment while 48.48% students considered it 'appropriate for both genders'. Not a single student considered it appropriate only for men. After the treatment the percentage of students considering Dress Designing 'appropriate for both genders' went up from 48.48% to 73.1% while the *F* score came down from 36.2% to 9%. The *M* score remained 0. Thus, after the treatment the profession of Dress Designer moved to the category 'appropriate for both but with a slight inclination towards women'.

TABLE 4.11 : Professions considered More Appropriate for Men

Professions included in the Category before Treatment	Change after Treatment		
	Noteworthy	Upto Some Extent	Negligible
Chef	Collector	Shopkeeper	Chef
Shopkeeper		Industrialist	Electrician
Electrician		Manager	
Collector		Architect	
Industrialist			
Manager			
Architect			

As shown in Table 4.11 seven professions were considered more appropriate for men. Before the treatment, at least 20%

students considered them 'appropriate only for men'. The *F* score was 0 for all seven professions. After the treatment negligible change was observed in two professions — Chef and Electrician. In fact, in the case of Electrician the *T* score came down by 4% and *M* score went up by 3%.

The professions for which the change was observed to some extent included : Shopkeeper (*T* score went up from 50.88% before treatment to 58.2% after treatment and *M* score came down from 33.9% to 25.4%); Industrialist (*T* score went up from 59.6% before treatment to 76.1% after treatment and *M* score came down from 21.76% to 6%); Manager (*T* score went up from 59.6% before treatment to 77.6% after treatment and *M* score came down from 19.4% to 4.5%); and Architect (*T* score went up from 58.4% to 79.1% and *M* score came down from 19.4% to 4.5%). Despite the change, the profession of Shopkeeper remained in the same category after treatment while Industrialist, Manager and Architect moved to the category 'appropriate for both genders but with a slight inclination towards men', but the extent of change was negligible.

Collector was the only profession on which noteworthy change was observed after treatment. The *T* score went up from 58.6% before treatment to 83.6% after treatment and the *M* score came down from 21.76% to 0. The *F* score remained 0 before and after treatment. Thus, after treatment the profession of Collector moved to the category 'appropriate for both, men and women'.

TABLE. 4.12 : Professions Considered Predominantly Feminine

Professions included in the Category before Treatment	Change after Treatment		
	Noteworthy	Upto Some Extent	Negligible
Baby-sitter	Housework	Baby-sitter	
Nurse		Nurse	
Housework		Pre-School Teacher	
Pre-school Teacher			

Table 4.12 shows four professions falling in the category of predominantly feminine professions before treatment. For these professions the percentages of students considering these professions 'appropriate only for women' were higher than those considering them appropriate for both genders.

After the treatment change up to some extent was observed on three professions — Baby-sitter (*T* score went up from 2.4% before treatment to 9.0% after treatment and *F* score came down from 82.4% to 74.6%); Nurse (*T* score went up from 12.16% before treatment to 20.9% after treatment and *F* score came down from 70.24% to 62.7%); and Pre-school teacher (*T* score went up from 40.3% before treatment to 52.2% after treatment and *F* score came down from 43.68% to 31.3%). In all three cases *M* score was 0 before as well as after treatment. Despite the change all three professions remained in the category of 'professions considered predominantly feminine'.

Housework was the only profession which registered noteworthy change after treatment. The *T* score went up from 14.6% before treatment to 38 per cent after treatment and *F* score came down from 70.2% to 43.3%. Housework, however, remained in the same category (that is, predominantly Feminine) even after the change.

TABLE 4.13 : Professions Considered Predominantly Masculine

Professions included in the Category before Treatment	Change after Treatment		
	Noteworthy	Upto Some Extent	Negligible
Taxi Driver	Waiter	Taxi Driver	Mechanic
Farmer	Pilot	Farmer	
Waiter			
Mechanic			
Pilot			

As shown in Table 4.13 five professions were in the category 'predominantly masculine' before treatment. For these professions the percentages of students considering them appropriate only for men were higher than those considering them appropriate for both genders.

After the treatment the change registered on the profession of Mechanic was negligible; the *T* score went up from 29.1% before treatment to 29.9% after treatment and the *M* score came down from 55.7% to 53.7%.

Taxi Driver and Farmer were two professions on which change up to some extent was observed. In case of Taxi Driver the *T* score rose from 7.2% before treatment to 19.4% after treatment while *M* score came down from 77.6% to 64.2%. In case of Farmer the *T* score rose from 7.2% before treatment to 25.4% after treatment and the *M* score came down from 75.2% to 58.2%. Despite the change both the professions remained in the same category— 'predominantly masculine'.

Noteworthy change was observed on two professions — Waiter and Pilot. In case of Pilot the *T* score went up from 38.7% before treatment to 67.2% after treatment and the *M* score came down from 46.1% to 16.4%. In case of Waiter the *T* score rose from 16.9% before treatment to 43.3% and the *M* score came down from 63.04% to 40.3%. Thus, after treatment the profession of Pilot shifted from the category 'predominantly masculine' to the category 'appropriate for both but with slight inclination towards men' that of Waiter moved to the category 'more appropriate for men'.

For all the five professions in this category the *F* score was 0 before as well as after treatment.

REASONS GIVEN FOR GENDER-STEREOTYPING PROFESSIONS

The gender-stereotype test required the respondents to give a reason when they marked a profession appropriate only for men or only for women.

Qualitative analysis revealed that all the reasons given by students fell into eight broad categories. There were several students who did not give any reason for their choice.

The categories are described below with examples (translated into English) from the response sheets.

(1) Category A

Reasons stating that a profession is appropriate for only men or only women because conventionally or traditionally they have been doing it.

Examples:

(i) Traditionally it is women's job.
(ii) Usually this job is handled by men.
(iii) This is women's duty.
(iv) This job is more suitable for men.
(v) Never saw a woman doing this job.
(vi) Not appropriate for males.
(vii) Only women have been doing this job.

(viii) The name of the job (e.g. nurse) itself suggests that it is meant for women.

(2) Category B

Reasons stating that only men or only women have the necessary knowledge, skills or art for a particular profession.

Examples:

(i) Women lack the knowledge required for this job.
(ii) Men do not have the appropriate skill for this job.
(iii) Women lack the know-how required for this job.
(iv) Only women possess the art of doing this.

(3) Category C

Reasons stating physical strength as a key factor in a particular profession (predominantly used in 'male' professions).

Examples:

(i) This job requires a strong physique.
(ii) Women lack the necessary strength.
(iii) Women are delicate.
(iv) Women cannot work under inclement weather conditions.
(v) This job requires hard work.

(4) Category D

Reasons stating that only men or only women have the innate qualities required for a particular profession.

Examples:

(i) This job is not suitable to male temperament.
(ii) A woman would be scared of doing such a job.
(iii) Women are more affectionate and caring.
(iv) Women lack the level of intelligence required.
(v) Women lack the necessary will-power.
(vi) Men lack the patience required.
(vii) Men are temperamentally harsh.

(5) Category E

Reasons stating socio-cultural factors (more frequently used in a negative way to show why a profession is not suitable for men or women).

Examples:

(i) Such a job will defame a woman.
(ii) This job is not befitting a man.
(iii) This job is below the dignity of men.
(iv) One's family would not permit taking up such a job.
(v) In such a job there is risk of molestation.
(vi) People may consider a holder of such a job a woman of easy virtue
(vii) The society will not accept a man/a woman in this job.
(viii) The person will be ridiculed by people.

(6) Category F

Reasons stating that men or women have other responsibilities which makes it difficult for them to take up a particular profession.

Examples:

(i) They have other responsibilities.

(ii) They are busy otherwise.

(7) Category G

Stating low income as a reason (chiefly used negatively to show why a profession is not appropriate for men).

Examples:

(i) This is a low paid job.
(ii) The remuneration is not adequate.

(8) Category H

Stating lack of opportunity as reason.

Examples:

(i) Women do not get opportunity to get this job.
(ii) Men are not chosen for this job.

Tables 4.41 to 4.17 present quantitative analysis of reasons given for different categories of professions.

TABLE 4.14 : Reasons Given for the Professions Considered More Appropriate for Women

(in percentages of respondents)

Reasons	Tradition Convention (A)		Knowledged Skill (B)		Physical Strength (C)		Innate Quality (D)		Social Reasons (E)		Other Respon-sibilities (F)		Low Income (G)		Lack of Opportunity (H)	
Test	Pre	Post	Pre	Post	Pre	Post	Pre	Post	Pre	Post	Pre	Post	Pre	Post	Pre	Post
Profession																
Fashion Model	12.2	7.6	19.4	6.0	—	—	19.4	1.5	12.2	9.1	—	—	—	—	—	—
Dress Designer	19.4	3.0	17.0	7.6	—	—	2.4	—	—	—	—	—	2.4	—	—	—
	31.6	10.6	36.4	13.6	0	0	21.8	1.5	12.2	9.1	0	0	2.4	0	0	0

TABLE 4.15 : Reasons Given for the Professions Considered Predominantly Feminine

(in percentages of respondents)

Reasons	Tradition Convention		Knowledge Skill		Physical Strength		Innate Quality		Social Reasons		Other Respon-sibilities		Low Income		Lack of Opportunity	
	(A)		(B)		(C)		(D)		(E)		(F)		(G)		(H)	
Test	Pre	Post	Pre	Post	Pre	Post	Pre	Post	Pre	Post	Pre	Post	Pre	Post	Pre	Post
Profession																
Babysitter	14.0	9.1	48.3	24.2	—	—	21.8	39.4	2.4	3.0	2.4	—	—	—	—	—
Nurse	31.5	30.3	7.2	9.1	—	—	17.0	15.2	12.2	6.1	—	—	2.4	—	—	1.5
Housework	19.0	22.7	36.3	3.0	—	—	—	—	21.8	13.6	4.8	3.0	—	—	—	—
Preschool Teacher	7.2	4.5	19.4	6.0	—	—	19.4	19.7	—	—	—	—	—	—	—	—
	71.7	66.6	111.2	42.3	0	0	58.2	74.3	36.4	22.7	7.2	3.0	2.4	0	0	1.5

TABLE 4.16 : Reasons Given for the Professions Considered More Appropriate for men

(in percentages of respondents)

Reasons	Tradition Convention (A)		Knowledge Skill (B)		Physical Strength (C)		Innate Quality (D)		Social Reasons (E)		Other Respon-sibilities (F)		Low Income (G)		Lack of Opportunity (H)	
Test	Pre	Post	Pre	Post	Pre	Post	Pre	Post	Pre	Post	Pre	Post	Pre	Post	Fre	Post
Profession																
Chef	14.0	16.7	11.8	1.5	7.2	3.0	—	—	4.8	12.1	—	—	2.3	—	—	—
Shopkeeper	7.2	7.6	14.6	7.6	—	—	—	—	12.2	10.6	—	—	—	—	—	—
Electrician	9.8	10.6	4.8	6.1	2.4	6.1	7.2	10.6	4.8	4.5	—	—	—	—	—	—
Collector	4.8	—	9.8	—	—	—	2.4	—	—	—	—	—	—	—	—	—
	35.8	34.9	41.0	15.2	9.6	9.1	9.6	10.6	21.8	27.2	0	0	2.3	0	0	0

TABLE 4.17 : Reasons Given for the Professions Considered Predominantly Masculine

(in percentages of respondents)

Reasons	Tradition Convention (A)		Knowledge Skill (B)		Physical Strength (C)		Innate Quality (D)		Social Reasons (E)		Other Respon-sibilities (F)		Low Income (G)		Lack of Opportunity (H)	
Test	Pre	Post	Pre	Post	Pre	Post	Pre	Post	Pre	Post	Pre	Post	Pre	Post	Pre	Post
Profession																
Taxi Drivers	19.4	10.6	7.2	4.5	2.4	6.1	7.2	19.7	34.0	21.2	2.4	—	2.4	—	—	1.5
Farmer	7.2	6.1	19.4	4.5	53.4	42.4	—	1.5	2.4	3.0	2.4	1.5	—	—	—	—
Waiter	12.2	12.1	12.2	—	2.3	—	—	1.5	36.3	24.2	—	—	4.8	—	—	1.5
Mechanic	12.2	18.2	29.2	9.0	17.0	16.7	—	3.0	2.4	7.6	—	—	—	—	—	—
Pilot	21.8	7.6	9.8	—	—	—	14.6	9.1	—	—	—	—	—	—	—	—
	72.8	54.6	72.8	18.0	75.1	65.2	21.8	34.8	75.1	56.0	4.8	1.5	7.2	0	0	3.0

TABLE 4.18 : Difference in Frequency of Reason Categories Before and After Treatment

Reason	Professions													
	1			2			3			4			Total	
	Predominantly Feminine			More Appropriate for Women			Predominantly Masculine			More Appropriate for Men				
Category	Before Treat-ment	After Treat-ment	Diffe-rence	Before Treat-ment	After Treat-ment	Diffe-rence	Before Treat-ment	After Treat-ment	Diffe-rence	Before Treat-ment	After Treat-ment	Diffe-rence	Before Treat-ment	After Treat-ment (% reduc-tion)
A. Tradition/ Convention	71.7	66.2	5.5	31.6	10.6	21.0 z	72.8	54.6	18.2	43.0	36.4	6.6	219.1	168.2 (23.2)
B. Knowledge, Skill, Art	111.2	42.3	68.9	36.4	13.6	22.8	72.8	18.0	54.	70.0	18.2	51.8	290.4	92.1 (68.3)
C. Physical Strength	0	0	0	0	0	0	75.1	65.2	9.9	14.4	10.6	3.8	88.0	76.1 (13.5)
D.Innate Quality	58.2	74.3	16.1*	21.8	1.5	20.3	21.8	34.8	13.0*	21.6	10.6	11.0	123.4	122.7 (0.01)
E. Social Reasons	36.4	22.7	13.7	12.2	9.1	3.1	75.1	56.0	19.1	36.2	30.2	6.0	160.0	118.0 (26.3)

(Contd.)

TABLE 4.18: *(Contd.)*

Reason	Professions 1 Predominantly Feminine			2 More Appropriate for Women			3 Predominantly Masculine			4 More Appropriate for Men			Total	
Category	Before Treatment	After Treatment	Difference	Before Treatment	After Treatment	Difference	Before Treatment	After Treatment	Difference	Before Treatment	After Treatment	Difference	Before Treatment	After Treatment (% reduction)
F. Other Responsibilities	7.2	3.0	4.2	0	0	0	4.8	1.5	2.5	0	0	0	12.0	4.5 (62.5)
G. Low Income Convention	2.4	0	2.4	2.4	0	2.4	0	2.4	7.2	0	7.2	2.3	14.3	0 (0)
H. Lack of Opportunities	0	1.5	1.5*	0	0	0	0	3	3*	0	0	0	0	4.5

* Percentage of the frequency before treatment.

Comments on Reasons given for Gender-Stereotyping Professions

(1) Before the treatment Knowledge, Skill, Art; Tradition/Convention; Social Reasons; and Innate Qualitics were the most frequently stated reasons (in descending order) for a profession being considered appropriate for only one gender. Also, the same categories of reasons were cited for majority of professions. After treatment also they remained the most frequcntly stated reasons but the order changed: Tradition/Convention; Innate Qualities; Social Reasons; and Knowledge, Skill, Art in descending order.

(2) When the reasons given before-treatment and after-treatment were compared, for every reason category except 'lack of opportunity' (the score increased from 0 to 4.5) the after-treatment frequency was lower than the before treatment frequency. The difference in frequencies was observed as shown in Table 4.18.
For professions considered predominantly feminine and masculine the after-treatment frequencies were higher than the before-treatment frequencies for the reason (Category D)innate qualities.

(3) The maximum difference in before-treatment and after-treatment frequencies was observed for the reason (Category B) (knowledge, skill and art) (reduction by 68.3%). Compared to that the difference is much less for categories 'tradition/ convention, (reduction by 23.2%) and, social reasons' (reduction by 26.3%) and the difference is the least for the category 'innate qualities' (reduction by 0.01%).

(4) Before-treatment and after-treatment (reduction by 13.5%) 'requirement of physical strength' was predominantly cited as a reason for the profession of farmer and to some extent for mechanic to explain why these professions are considered appropriate only for men. Understandably, the justification of physical strength was given for only those professions having a masculine inclination.

(5) 'Other responsibilities at home' are in reality a factor which discourages many women from taking up certain professions which demand long hours or very high responsibility at a job. Remarkably, negligible percentage of students thought of this factor. A very small percentage considered it while justifying why men cannot do baby sitting or housework.

(6) Lack of opportunity is also a major constraint for both genders in taking up unconventional professions. But students considering this factor were again negligible in percentage. None of the students gave this reason before the treatment and only 4.5% after the treatment.

CHANGE IN VALUE JUDGEMENT

The Value Test was in two parts : Part-I was scored quantitatively and analysed statistically while Part-II was subjected to qualitative analysis.

Comparison of Adjusted Mean Value Judgement of Experimental Group and of Control Group

Adjusted mean value judgement of the experimental group was compared with that of the control group. Comparison was made by considering the pretest scores of the same variable as Co-variate and data were analysed using ANCOVA. Table 4.19 summarises the results of ANCOVA.

TABLE 4.19 : Summary of ANCOVA for Value Judgement taking Treatment as a Source of Variance

Source of Variance	df	SSy.x	MSSy.x	Fy.x
Treatment	1	133.903	133.903	5.020*
Error	89	2374.206	26.676	

* Significant at 0.05 level.

Table 4.19 shows that the adjusted F-value is significant at 0.05 level. It indicates that the effect of the treatment on the two groups with respect to value judgement differed significantly.

TABLE 4.20 : Testwise Mean, SE and *t*-Value of Value Judgement in the Control Group and in the Experimental Group

Control Group					Experimental Group				
Test	Mean	SE	r	*t*-value	Test	Mean	SE	r	*t*-value
Pre-Test	27.71	0.93	0.896	1.03	Pre-Test	28.02	0.65	0.58	4.52**
Post-Test	28.32	1.25			Post-Test	30.55	0.57		

** Significant at 0.01 level.

Table 4.20 shows the sample means and SE of the pretest and posttest scores and the *t*-value for the control and the experimental groups.

Table 4.20 shows that the mean pretest and posttest value judgement scores do not differ significantly in the control group but the difference is significant in the experimental group. It indicates that value discussion model as treatment significantly affected value judgement of students in the experimental group. The scores in the experimental group also indicate that the effect was in the positive direction.

The value test contained twelve situations (Appendix 4). Correlated *t*-test/paired samples *t*-test was carried out for the experimental group taking the mean pretest score and mean posttest score on each of the twelve situations.

Table 4.21 shows the testwise mean, SE and *t*-value of Value Judgement for the seven situations on which the mean posttest scores significantly differed from the mean pretest scores.

Table 4.22 shows the testwise Mean, SE and *t*-value of Value Judgement for the five situations on which the mean pretest and posttest scores did not differ significantly.

The second part of the response on value test required students to give justifications for their choice of a particular alternative. The different reasons given for each choice under every situation were summarised and tabulated in terms of the frequency of their justification before treatment and after treatment to see if there was any shift due to treatment.

TABLE 4.21: Testwise Mean, SE and t-Value of Value Judgement for Situations on which Value Discussion Model was found Effective

Situation on value test	Test	Mean	SE	r	t-value
Situation - 2	Pretest	1.53	0.124		
A boy applying for Home Science				0.459	3.45**
	Posttest	1.98	0.129		
Situation - 3	Pretest	2.26	0.135		
Husband of a working woman sharing household work				0.573	2.08*
	Posttest	2.50	0.113		
Situation - 4	Pretest	1.88	0.117		
Who to entertain guests — brother watching tele-vision or sister doing school lessons?				0.363	2.12*
	Posttest	2.15	0.111		
Situation - 5	Pretest	2.14	0.138		
Brothers sharing home-chores with sisters after school				0.303	1.93*
	Posttest	2.42	0.112		
Situation - 8	Pretest	1.76	0.137		
Dress-code for daughter-in-law				0.349	3.93**
	Posttest	2.33	0.119		
Situation - 9	Pretest	2.21	0.137		
Partiality in punish-ment to boys and girls				0.201	2.09*
	Posttest	2.55	0.113		

* Significant at 0.05 level.
** Significant at 0.01 level.

TABLE 4.22: Testwise Mean, SE and t-Value of Value Judgement for Situations on which Value Discussion Model had No Significant Effect

Situation on value test	Test	Mean	SE	r	t-value
Situation - 1	Pretest	1.65	0.132		
Girls expected to cook for the				0.435	1.18
group on a picnic	Posttest	1.81	0.133		
Situation - 6	Pretest	2.37	0.131		
Priority for a bright girl student-betrothal or advanced				0.354	1.00
education	Posttest	2.52	0.106		
Situation - 7	Pretest	2.27	0.137		
Cooking classes for girls and Karate classes for boys in summer				0.260	0.56
vacation	Posttest	2.36	0.127		
Situation - 10	Pretest	2.53	0.128		
Taking part in the crusade against social				0.236	1.27
evils	Posttest	2.71	0.101		
Situation - 11	Pretest	2.77	0.396		
Special bus for working				0.110	0.08
women	Posttest	2.74	0.097		

Note : Except Situation No. 1, the pretest scores were already high on all situations especially on nos. 10 and 11. The maximum Mean Score possible on the pretest and posttest on any situation being 3, one can see why the statistical analysis shows no significant change in the posttest.

SITUATION 1

I. You have gone for mountaineering with your friends. After reaching your destination you come to know that the organizers have not hired a cook. The organizers argue that in the group there are many girls who can cook after completing the day's mountaineering which would help cut down the expenditure and the group members will have to bear less costs per head.

	Frequency	
	Before treat-ment	After treat-ment
Choice-1		
You agree with the organizers and you will support their argument.		
Category 1.1	6	4
* At home it is girls' job to cook, why then should they have objection to cook when on outing? (boys and girls)	/	/
* If the girls are not to cook, who will? (boys and girls)	/	/
* Girls need not feel ashamed in cooking, need they? (boys and girls)	/	/
* If the hiker group has some girls as members, where is the need of engaging a cook? (boys and girls)	/	/
Category 1.2	4	3
* Boys are no match to girls in preparing tasty dishes. (boys and girls)	—	/
* Cooking will afford the girls training for the future. (girls)	—	/
* Such an arrangement will be convenient to all. (boys and girls)	/	—

(Contd.)

SITUATION 1 : *(Contd.)*

	Frequency	
	Before treat-ment	After treat-ment
Category 1.3	10	15
* Expenditure will be less. The resulting savings (if a cook is not engaged) will enable the group to have extended sight seeing. (boys and girls)	_/	_/
* From the savings the girls can prepare additional tasty dishes which should be a delight to the boys. (boys)	_/	_/
Category 1.4	5	9
* Self-cooking is a pleasant activity which can give tasty dishes. (boys and girls)	_/	_/
* It is our duty to give co-operation. (girls)	_/	_/
* We shall remain hungry if we indulge in this sort of argumentation. (girls)	_/	—
* We must help our team-mates and cooperate with friends. (girls)	—	_/
* Working with and for friends is more pleasant than even mountaineering. (girls)	_/	_/
* We have to listen to the organizers who are in control. (boys)	_/	—
Category 1.5	0	1
* Let the girls cook for the group, but we shall compel the organizers to monetarily compensate the group for not engaging a cook. (a boy)	—	_/

SITUATION 1 : *(Contd.)*

	Frequency	
	Before treatment	After treatment
Choice 2 : You do not agree with the organizers but you will keep quiet.		
Category 2.1	11	2
* Protesting will spoil the atmosphere; better to do the assigned job remaining silent. (girls)	√	—
* Anyway it is we who cook at home; we are prepared to take up cooking here also. (girls)	√	—
* We shall protest a little bit and thereafter cook for the group after resting for a while. (girls)	√	—
* (If we do not cook) are we going to remain hungry? (girls)	√	—
* Protesting will not get us a cook. (a girl)	—	√
* Why argue as if we can go back to the base to get a cook? (a girl)	—	√
Choice 3 You do not agree with the organizers and you will openly oppose their decision.		
Category 3.1	16	12
* The girls have paid for the tour as much as the boys; if they are required to undertake cooking, their money would go waste. (boys and girls)	√	√
* The girls have joined the group for sight seeing, pleasure and relaxation, what pleasure will they get if cooking is forced on them? (boys and girls)	√	√

SITUATION 1: *(Contd.)*

	Frequency	
	Before treat-ment	After treat-ment
* The girls have to cook at home. If they have to take up the same duty here also, how can they feel the pleasure of changing the routine? (boys and girls)	✓	✓
* Girls are not bound to accept cooking as a permanent duty. (boys and girls)	—	✓
* Why should the girls be expected to accept drudgery to bring down the tour expenses for the whole group? (girls)	✓	✓
Category 3.2	*2*	*0*
* After practising mountain-climbing we shall be tired and hungry as wolves. If the girls are to cook after coming down, they will take time in cooking. We might, then feel inclined to engage in destructive activities driven by pangs of hunger. (boys)	✓	—

Choice 4
Any other option.

Category 4.1	3	1
* If the girls are expected to cook, the boys must be assigned other duties. (girls)	✓	✓
* If the girls have to cook, the boys must be assigned the job of cleaning utensils. (girls)	✓	—
Category 4.2	8	20
* Now that it is not possible to get a cook we boys will help the girls in cooking. (boys)	✓	✓

SITUATION 1: *(Contd.)*

	Frequency	
	Before treat-ment	After treat-ment
* In mountain-climbing the girls get tired as much as the boys. It would be injustice to girls if they alone have to cook for the group. The boys and girls should cooperate with each other in cooking. (boys and girls)	_/	_/
Category 4.3	0	1
* It is the organizers who are at fault and it is they who shall help the girls in cooking. (a boy)		

_/ shows whether the reasoining was given before or after the treatment or at both the times.

Observations

The reasons given in support of various choices vary from low level (favouring *status quo*, blindly respecting the authority or motivated by personal benefit) to higher levels demanding logical justice and a practical but just way-out. Even though a large number of respondents continued favouring the *status quo* reflecting gender bias (resulting in the change being statistically insignificant), the rise (from 8 before the treatment to 20 after treatment in Category 4.2) in the number of respondents insisting for justice without gender bias and, at the same time, for working out a practical way-out of the unfavourable situation, indicates an encouraging influence of the treatment on some students.

SITUATION 2

II. Your younger brother has just passed his H.S.C. examination with good marks. He wants to join the Home Science College but the College refuses to accept boys. Your brother wants to take action against such a policy but does not receive much support at home or from friends. Under the circumstances —

	Frequency	
	Before treatment	After treatment
Choice 1 You will tell your brother that his choice is inappropriate and will advise him to choose some other discipline.		
Category 1.1	35	15
* Home Science is not an appropriate choice for boys. (boys and girls)	✓	✓
* What is there for a boy to learn in Home Science? (boys and girls)	✓	✓
* Home Science is meant for girls. (boys and girls)	✓	✓
* In Home Science they teach only household chores. (boys and girls)	✓	✓
* What job can a boy get after getting a degree in Home Science? (boys and girls)	✓	—
* As adults the boys are expected to earn and maintain parents, not to help in the kitchen. (girls)	✓	—
* A boy should go in for a paying line (like Chartered Accountancy) for a bright future. (boys and girls)	✓	✓
* Why should the boys poke their noses in a college meant only for girls? (girls)	—	✓

(Contd.)

SITUATION 2 : *(Contd.)*

	Frequency	
	Before treatment	After treatment
* Our Government is not entirely senseless. It must have felt that Home Science is not for boys and deny boys admission to Home Science. (girls)	√	—
* These days even girls do not prefer Home Science. Why should then boys take up Home Science? (girls)	√	√
* If admission to Home Science is made open for boys also, the chance of admission for girls will come down. (girls)	—	√
* Boys will be discredited if they take up jobs meant for girls. (boys and girls)	√	√
Choice-2		
You do not mind your brother's choice but you will not involve yourself in his crusade against the college.		
Category 2.1	4	2
* My brother's crusade against the college will harm the education of other college students. (boys and girls)	√	—
* How can we take steps against the college without knowing their difficulties? (a girl)	√	√
* How can a college be expected to change rules just for a solitary boy? (a boy)	—	√
Category 2.2	10	13
* We would not like to involve ourselves in a court case. (boys and girls)	√	√
* There is no end to disputes. (boys and girls)	√	√

(Contd.)

SITUATION 2: *(Contd.)*

	Frequency	
	Before treat-ment	After treat-ment
* I can't help my brother, but his friends can. boys)	_/	_/
* Even if my brother's choice is correct, what can be done against the rules? (boys and girls)	_/	_/
* It is no use taking up a fight against powers. (boys and girls)	_/	_/
* The fight against the college will result only in waste of time. (boys and girls)	_/	_/
* My brother should try for admission to Home Science in another city. (boys and girls)	_/	_/

Choice-3
You support your brother's choice and will help him take action against the college.

Category 3.1	6	11
* Which scripture restricts Home Science to only girls? (girls)	—	_/
* Either keep reserved seats for boys in Home Science Colleges or open Home Science Colleges for boys. (boys)	—	_/
* The word 'Home' in Home Science does not necessarily restrict admission to girls only. (boys and girls)	_/	_/
* This is injustice. I am prepared to support my brother even if we have to approach a High Court. (a boy)	_/	_/
* No work should be considered inferior. My brother will give lead to others by taking up Home Science. (a girl)	—	_/

(Contd.)

SITUATION 2: *(Contd.)*

	Frequency	
	Before treat-ment	After treat-ment
* The management should know that boys cannot harass girls if admitted to Home Science. These days girls are bold. (girls)	_/	_/
Category 3.2		
	12	20
* If girls can take up Engineering, why should the boys be denied Home Science? (boys and girls).	_/	_/
* If girls are permitted to select lines meant for boys, boys also should have similar right in selecting a career. (boys and girls)	—	_/
* In these days of equality of genders the rules for admission also must be the same for them. (boys and girls)	_/	_/
* Every individual should enjoy the right of going for education according to one's interest. (boys and girls)	_/	_/

_/ shows whether the reasoning was given before or after the treatment or at both the times.

Observations

There is an overall drift in the position of the respondents vis-a-vis gender-bias from conventional acceptance of separate male and female domains to the acceptance, may be to varying degrees, of gender-equality and logical justice.

The noteworthy point is that with respect to the Category 3.2 (showing higher quality of the justification for acceptance of gender-equality) the change in frequency is from 12 (before the treatment) to 20 (after the treatment).

SITUATION 3

III. You live with your parents and two elder brothers. One of your brothers is married. He and your *Bhabhi* (sister-in-law) work in the same office. They have a small daughter. Your *Bhabhi* does the household work before leaving for office and also cooks dinner after she comes back. She expects that your brother should share the childcare and household responsibilities but your parents do not like this at all as they think men are not expected to attend to such work.

	Frequency	
	Before treat-ment	After treat-ment
Choice 1		
You believe that the stand taken by your brother and parents is appropriate and you will support them.		
Category 1.1	4	1
* If the sister-in-law shows understanding and leaves her job the parents-in-law will be pleased. (boys and girls)	✓	—
* The *Bhabhi* (brother's wife) should finish home chores before going for her job or leave her job if she cannot manage. If I have my way I would make my *Bhabhi* leave her job. (a boy)	✓	✓
Category 1.2	8	6
* My brother will be put to ridicule by the society if he attends to the household chores. (boys)	✓	✓
* Household chores are women's job. (boys and girls)	✓	✓
* These days no man will be ready to do household chores. (a boy)	✓	—
* It is a shame that men have to attend to household chores when women are around. The *Bhabhi* should elicit help from mother-in-law and sister-in-law by love and tact. (boys and girls)	✓	✓

(Contd.)

SITUATION 3 : *(Contd.)*

	Frequency	
	Before treat-ment	After treat-ment
* In society there are many women who attend to both the household duties and outside job. (boys and girls)	/	/
* Someone has to cook in a home. (boys and girls)	—	/
* A woman compels her husband to do household work just to satisfy her ego. (a boy)	/	/
Choice 2 You agree with your *Bhabhi* but will keep quiet in the matter.		
Category 2.1	4	6
* The brother has to attend his office work. How can he be expected to help in household chores? My mother and I will help *Bhabhi* if she feels tired. (a girl)	—	/
* Even if I am in agreement with my *Bhabhi*, no one in the family will listen to me. My intervention will result only in loss of peace at home. (a boy and a girl)	/	/
* We juniors can't say anything to elders. (boys and girls)	—	/
* My brother will be displeased if I express my views. (a boy)	/	/
* My brother and *Bhabhi* should have considered such matters before marriage. (a boy)	/	—
* I don't like this tussel, but what can we do in this matter when God has ordained that women are to do household chores? (a girl)	/	/

(Contd.)

SITUATION 3 : *(Contd.)*

	Frequency	
	Before treat-ment	After treat-ment
Choice 3 You will take your *Bhabhi*'s side and try to convince your brother and parents that your *Bhabhi*'s expectations are reasonable.		
Category 3.1	20	23
* It is injustice to impose a double burden on *Bhabhi*. (boys and girls)	✓	✓
* *Bhabhi* is a human being, not a machine. (boys and girls)	✓	✓
* *Bhabhi* will get tired with the double burden. (boys and girls)	✓	✓
* *Bhabhi* will have mental tension. (boys and girls)	✓	✓
Category 3.2	8	11
* These days a man should not feel ashamed in taking up household chores. (boys and a girls)	—	✓
* If men can cook in hotels, why not at home? (girl)	—	✓
* The parents are old-fashioned, but what about the brother? He belongs to the modern times. (girls)	—	✓
* If the women do not feel ashamed in working outside, why should the men be ashamed of household work? (boys and girls)	✓	✓

(Contd.)

SITUATION 3 : *(Contd.)*

	Frequency Before treat-ment	After treat-ment
Category 3.3	23	29
* Husband and wife are called 'life-partners'. The word itself suggests that they should support and co-operate with each other in every aspect. (a boy)	—	✓
* By earning *Bhabhi* is reducing my brother's financial burden; he should also reciprocate (boys and girls)	✓	✓
* *Bhabhi* understands her own responsibility towards the family so all other family members should understand theirs and do their own work. (boys and girls)	✓	✓
* They both work equally hard at their jobs so they should do equal work at home also. (boys and girls)	✓	✓
Category 3.4	4	2
* How would we feel if we have to face similar situation in future? (girls)	✓	✓
* If your own daughter is given such a treatment, how would you feel? (girls)	✓	✓

Choice 4
Any other option.

* I understand *Bhabhi's* difficulty but I may not be able to argue so if no one helps, I will offer all the possible help to my *Bhabhi*. (a boy)	7 ✓	7 ✓

(Contd.)

SITUATION 3 : *(Contd.)*

	Frequency	
	Before treat-ment	After treat-ment
* It is true that *Bhabhi* gets tired so other women (mother/sister) in the family should help her. (boy and girl)	/	/
* Brother should not work in the kitchen but he can help in cleaning the house or fetching milk. (a girl)	/	/
* If brother has no skill in household chores one cannot force him, but he can look after the child. (a girl)	—	/
* We will hire a servant or a housemaid. (a boy)		/
* I will tell my brother that either he helps or ask *Bhabhi* to quit her job. I do not want quarrels in my house. (a boy)	/	—
* Brother should help *Bhabhi* but he should not help too much. (a boy)	/	—

Observations

The number of respondents choosing Choice-1 (more or less hardliners steeped in traditional gender bias) decreased after treatment. Also, as response to Choice-3 shows the number of respondents opting for gender equality and natural justice increased after treatment, as confirmed also by statistical analysis (Table 4.21).

The number of respondents choosing Choice-3.3 should be noted. Here the respondents have accepted gender equality and considered husband and wife as equal partners. The number of respondents which was 23 before treatment increased to 29 after treatment.

SITUATION 4

IV. Your parents have gone out leaving the charge of the house with you. In the evening some guests drop in. You have to carry on conversation with the guests. Your younger sister is doing her home-work while your younger brother is watching television. Whom would you ask to prepare tea and offer snacks to the guests?

	Frequency	
	Before treat-ment	After treat-ment
Choice 1 Ask younger sister to prepare tea and offer snacks to the guests.		
Category 1.1	7	5
* Brother would not know how to make tea. (boys and girls)	✓	✓
* If my brother makes tea and does not do a proper job of it, the guests would carry bad impression about our family. (a girl)	✓	✓
* Brother is too young. (boys and a girls)	✓	✓
Category 1.2	5	3
* I just don't like the idea that boys do household work. (a girl)	✓	✓
* Homework can wait. (boys and a girls)	✓	✓
* If the girl sits in the drawing room and the boy makes tea in the kitchen, what would the guests think? (a girl)	✓	✓
Category 1.3	12	27
* Homework cannot be disturbed; TV watching can wait. (boys and girls)	✓	✓
* Homework is more important. (boys and girls)	✓	✓

(Contd.)

SITUATION 4 : *(Contd.)*

	Frequency	
	Before treatment	After treatment
Category 1.4	1	3
* If girls can do boy's work, boys can do girl's work. (girls)	✓	✓
* Boys should be trained in chores like preparing tea. (girls)	—	✓
Choice 3 You will not offer tea or snacks to the guests under the pretext that parents are not at home.		
Choice 4 Any other alternative.	2	2
Category 4.1	2	5
* Younger brother will make tea but if he needs help, we sisters would go in the kitchen now and then to help him. (girls)	✓	✓
Category 4.2	1	1
* I will order readymade snacks. (a boy)	✓	✓
Category 4.3		
* I will prepare tea myself	24	7
— because I am elder and responsible. (boys and girls)	✓	✓
— because my parents have left the charge of the house to me. (boys and girls)	✓	✓
— guests can watch TV. (boys and girls)	✓	✓
— brother and sister will continue conversation with guests. (boys and girls)	✓	✓

(Contd.)

Observations

There is a general tendency towards decrease in gender-bias, which is especially seen in the case of Choice 2.1 where the number of respondents standing for equal and equitable treatment of girls and boys jumps from 12 (before treatment) to 27 (after treatment). Also the escapist tendency seen in the respondents opting for Category 4.3 the frequency after the treatment has dropped from 24 to 7.

SITUATION 5

V. You live in a joint family. In your family there is a tradition that after coming back from school girls have to help in house-work, while boys go out to play.

	Frequency	
	Before treatment	After treatment
Choice 1 You will oppose the tradition and will try to change it (how?)		
Category 1.1	32	27
* Today girls are equal to boys in every field (Slogan!) (boys and girls)	_/	_/
* Girls should have equal right to play (general) (boys and girls)	_/	_/
* Even we girls like to play after school (personal) (girls)	_/	_/
* It is not a crime to be born as a girl (boys)	_/	_/
* We sisters study as well as our brothers (girls)	_/	_/
* We girls also get tired and we also need to relax after school (girls)	_/	_/
* Should the boys be pampered just because they are born males? (girls)	_/	_/
* If my brother is supposed to work and earn when he grows up; so am I, so why should I help in housework? (girls)	_/	_/
* When girls grow up and get married they have to do housework. At least let them play now. (boys and girls)	_/	_/

(Contd.)

SITUATION 5 : *(Contd.)*

	Frequency	
	Before treat-ment	After treat-ment
* If boys do not help in housework, girls also won't help. (boys and girls)	✓	✓
* This is a gross in justice. (boys and girls)	—	✓
* Girls are also human. (boys and girls)	—	✓
* Housework hampers a girl's development and progress in studies. (boys and girls)	✓	✓
Category 1.2	2	2
* If girls do not play, boys also should not be allowed to play. (girls)	✓	✓
* Both should not play. (girls)	✓	✓
Category 1.3	8	20
* Boys and girls should study equally, play equally and offer equal help in housework. (girls)	—	✓
* I do not say that you reverse the rules but both boys and girls should play a little and help at home. (boys and girls)	✓	✓
* Helping in housework is also a boy's duty as much as a girl's. (boys and girls)	—	✓
* Training in household chores should be a a part of training for girls as well as boys. (boys and girls)	✓	✓
* We boys will help our sisters. (boys)	—	✓

(Contd.)

SITUATION 5 : *(Contd.)*

	Frequency	
	Before treat-ment	After treat-ment
Category 1.4	5	4
* Girls should be allowed to play a little after school. After that they should help in housework. (boys)		
Choice 2		
You do not like the tradition but you will keep quiet about it.		
Category 2.1	5	2
* Nobody will listen to us so better keep quiet. (boys and girls)	_/	—
* Youngers in the family have to respect elders' wishes. (boys and girls)	—	_/
* When I protest against such things I always get scolded by my parents and grandparents. (girls)	_/	—
* We have to keep quiet now but when we grow up we will change this tradition. (boys and girls)	_/	_/
Category 2.2	5	2
* Better keep quiet to please parents. (girls)	_/	—
* There is no point in arguing because parents always take brother's side. (girls)	—	_/
* Parents will be on my brother's side because when they grow old he is going to support and take care of them. (girls)	_/	—
* If I protest my parents would think that I am not obedient and I do not like to work. (girls)	—	_/

(Contd.)

SITUATION 5 : *(Contd.)*

	Frequency	
	Before treatment	After treatment
* If I protest, all the elders would say, "He is a boy after all but what will be your plight when you go to your in-laws? (girls)	/	—
Choice 3 You do not find anything wrong with the tradition and will let it continue.	12	6
* In future girls will have to take care of housework; not boys. (girls)	/	/
* Girls' jobs are to be done by girls. (boys and girls)	/	/
* When sisters are at home, why should brothers work? (girls)	/	—
* It would not be good if a girl is not trained in housework. Besides, girls get tired if they play. (boys)	/	—
* It is the accepted social norm that only girls do housework. (boys and girls)	/	/
* Girls in our family never object to doing housework. (boys)	—	/
* When they grow up girls are going to do housework whereas brother is going to earn and support parents. (girls)	/	/
* It is our duty to help our mother. (girls)	/	/
Choice 4 Any other alternative.	3	3
* Girls should help in housework after school and boys should sit down to study. No one needs to play. (girls)	—	/

(Contd.)

SITUATION 5 : *(Contd.)*

	Frequency	
	Before treat-ment	After treat-ment
* Elders should do all the housework and not bother children. (boys)	/	/
* Boys can help in jobs like shopping. (girls)	/	/
* Boys should not be forced to help in house-work but if they have some sense they would offer help. (girls)	/	—

Observations

In case of Choice 1, the respondents offering Category 1.1 are apparently influenced by cliches or show emotional outburst against an existing social situation based on gender-bias. Here the frequency (after treatment) changes to 27 from 32. Maybe some of the respondents opted for more rational Choice after the treatment and moved to Category 1.3, which is based on equitable and practical considerations. (In Category 1.3 the frequency jumped to 20 after treatment from 8 before treatment.)

There is also a decrease in the number of boys and girls who accept gender-equality but are too timid to stand up against tradition.

Responses opting for Choice 3 also show decrease in number from 12 to 6 after treatment.

SITUATION 6

VI. Your elder sister is a very bright student. She graduated this year and she has been engaged to a graduate young man from your community. Your sister desires to study for a post-graduate degree but the boy's family is not in favour of it. If your sister studies further the betrothal may be terminated. Under the circumstances—

	Frequency	
	Before treat-ment	After treat-ment
Choice 1		
You will support your sister's wish for further studies.		
Category 1.1	9	9
* If boys can study further after marriage, girls can too. (girls)	—	✓
* A girl should be free to make her own decision. (boys and girls)	✓	✓
* If a bright girl wants to study further, she should fulfil her desire. (boys and girls)	✓	✓
Category 1.2	20	32
* Studies are more important than marriage. (boys and girls)	✓	✓
* In today's world those who do not study repent. (boys and girls)	✓	✓
* Uneducated people have no place in today's world. (boys and girls)	✓	✓
* If a girl is educated her future is bright. (boys and girls)	✓	✓
* If my sister will study well, she will be able to face life independently. (boys and girls)	✓	✓

(Contd.)

SITUATION 6 : *(Contd.)*

	Frequency	
	Before treatment	After treatment
* If she is educated she can solve problems in future. (boys and girls)	✓	✓
* Education will develop her potential. (boys and girls)	—	✓
* If she studies she can take up a job in future and earn; whereas if she gets married she will do housework all her life. (boys and girls)	✓	✓
Category 1.3	12	24
* If my sister is well-educated and capable of earning she will get another, perhaps a better proposal in future. (boys and girls)	✓	✓
* My sister should not worry about broken engagement and concentrate on studies. (boys and girls)	✓	✓
Category 1.4	3	3
* In-laws have no right to stop a girl's education. (boys and girls)	✓	✓
* If her in-laws break engagement, it proves that in future they cannot make my sister happy. (boys and girls)	✓	✓
Category 1.5	1	1
* It is a wrong notion that the husband has to be more educated than wife. (a girl)	✓	✓
Category 1.6	*0*	*1*
* One should study to one's heart's desire in young age. It is difficult to study later. (a girl)	—	✓

SITUATION 6 : *(Contd.)*

	Frequency	
	Before treat-ment	After treat-ment
Choice 2		
You will persuade your sister to take up something like tailoring or dress-design instead of going for a Master's degree.	10	10
* She can do something interesting without displeasing her in-laws. (boys and girls)	/	/
* A broken engagement can be disastrous for her. (boys and girls)	/	/
* A broken engagement brings bad name to the girl and also to her family. (boys and girls)	/	/
* If the boy is good, a middle way is better. (boys and girls)	/	/
* It is not easy to find a good match again. (boys and girls)	/	/
* If she cultivates some other interest, parents would be happy and also her in-laws. (boys and girls)	/	/
Choice 3		
You will persuade your sister to abandon her idea of studying further and get married.	4	4
* My sister should get married and obey her in-laws' wishes. (a boy)	/	—
* Getting a good husband is more important than education for a happy life. (a girl)	/	/
* Later her in-laws might understand and let her study. (a girl)	/	/

SITUATION 6 : *(Contd.)*

	Frequency	
	Before treat-ment	After treat-ment
* If her in-laws are not in favour of further education, it is obvious that they will not let her take up a job in future. What is the use of getting a Master's degree in such a situation? (a boy and a girl)	—	/
* One has to obey elders. (boys and girls)	/	/

Observations

The number of the conservatives, rigid (Choice 3) or a bit liberal (Choice 2) has remained relatively small. The change opting for gender-equality is seen in far greater number of cases (Choice 1, Categories 1.2 and 1.3) 32 against 20 and 24 against 12 after the treatment. This shows the trend, though statistical analysis does not show significance (Table 4.22).

SITUATION 7

VII. You are a member of the Youth Club of your community. The Club has planned to organise summer vacation courses for members. With a large majority it has been decided to conduct Cookery classes for girls and Karate classes for boys. Parents also whole-heartedly support the plan.

	Frequency	
	Before treatment	After treatment
Choice 1		
You agree with the club's plan.		
Category 1.1	11	9
* The classes are planned according to natural interests of boys and girls. (boys and girls)	✓	✓
* Boys will need Karate skills in future and girls would need cooking skills. (boys and girls)	✓	✓
* Cooking classes will improve girls' cooking; they will get more respect from their in-laws. (boys)	✓	✓
Category 1.2	4	0
* One has to respect the decision of the majority. (boys and girls)	✓	—
* Whatever elders decide is for our good. (boys and girls)	✓	—
Choice 2		
You do not agree with the club's plan and will be vocal about it.		
Category 2.1	9	17.
* Girls can be interested in cooking as well as Karate. (boys and girls)	✓	✓
* Girls should also learn Karate for self-protection. (boys and girls)	✓	✓

(Contd.)

SITUATION 7 : *(Contd.)*

	Frequency	
	Before treatment	After treatment
* I like Karate so I will not let myself be forced to join cooking classes. (girl)	—	√
Category 2.2	38	40
* There should be no discrimination between boys and girls. (boys and girls)	√	√
* Both boys and girls should be allowed to pursue their interest for their better development. (boys and girls)	√	√
* Both, cooking and Karate, can be useful to boys as well as girls. (boys and girls)	√	√
* Today you see instances that wife goes out to work and husband looks after home. (boys and girls)	√	√
* If you take my example, I like cooking and Karate equally. (a boy)	√	√
* If girls learn Karate it can be useful for self-protection and when a boy works abroad or when he is alone at home he can benefit from the skills learnt in cooking classes. (boys and girls)	√	—
* Today we see in Zee TV that Men cook in programmes like "Khana Khazana" whereas girls are seen on many Karate programmes. (a boy)	—	√

Observations

Though there is a definite change resulting in decreased number with marked gender bias (Choice 1), a noteworthy point is that the change to decreased number showing gender bias took place at lower level (Choice 2; Category 2.1), the higher level response (Choice 2; Category 2.2) not increasing its numerical strength substantially (only 40 from 38) after treatment; probably because it was already high.

SITUATION 8

VIII. Your elder brother has recently got married. Your *Bhabhi* likes to wear Salwar-Kameez, midi-skirt etc. which are in current fashion. In your family daughters are allowed to wear such dresses but the daughter-in-law is supposed to wear only the traditional Sari. The elders in the family are very strict about the dress code. Under the circumstances —

	Frequency	
	Before treat-ment	After treat-ment
Choice 1		
You will support the elders.	28	14
* It is the tradition of our society. (boys and girls)	_/	_/
* The daughter-in-law is the custodian of the family honour. (boys and girls)		
* The new daughter-in-law has to form good impression on her in-laws so it is better to wear Sari. (girls)	_/	_/
* Only Sari is the proper dress for the daughter-in-law. (boys and girls)		
* If some elders visit, the daughter-in-law should present an easily identifiable respectable image. (boys and girls)	_/	_/
* People will talk about it and it will bring bad name to family. (boys and girls)	_/	_/
* There are young boys/men in the family who may not form a flippant image of the daughter-in-law. (a boy)	_/	—
* Even if a girl is a daughter of our family, I would insist that she should wear only Sari if she is at her in-laws' place. (a girls)	_/	—

(Contd.)

SITUATION 8 : *(Contd.)*

	Frequency	
	Before treatment	After treatment
* It would have been a different matter if the daughter-in-law were living in U.S.A. (boys and girls)	/	—
* Wearing Sari is a duty of every married Hindu woman. (boys and girls)	/	—
* A married woman cannot present herself in front of elders in any other dress but Sari. (boys and girls)	/	—
* A married woman must observe the behaviour code set by her society. (boys and girls)	/	—
* A daughter-in-law should obey and respect the elders of the family. (boys and girls)	/	/
* When a girl is allowed all sorts of freedom of wearing dresses when young, why should she crave for something against the social norms after marriage? (a girl)	—	/
Choice 2		
You feel that the elders are being unfair but would prefer to keep quiet.	6	3
* Orthodox elders will not listen to a youngster like me. (boys)	/	/
* It does not look proper if youngsters poke their noses in such affairs. (boys and girls)	/	/
Choice 3		
You will take your *Bhabhi*'s side and pressurise the elders to change.		
Category 3.1	13	25
* Mummy's time was different. Old customs must change. (boys and girls)	/	/

(Contd.)

SITUATION 8 : *(Contd.)*

	Frequency	
	Before treatment	After treatment
* Times have changed today. (boys and girls)	✓	✓
* In other countries and even in some families in our country everyone wears all kinds of dresses. (boys and girls)	✓	✓
* Everyone should have right to dress according to one's choice. (boys and girls)	✓	✓
* This is an injustice. (boys and girls)	—	✓
* Impropriety lies in the eyes of the observer, not in the dress. (a boy)	—	✓
Category 3.2	12	27
* If a daughter can wear all kinds of dresses why not a daughter-in-law? (boys and girls)	✓	✓
* The daughter-in-law should be treated like a daughter. (boys and girls)	✓	✓
* If our sister gets married and her in-laws force her to wear only Sari, won't she feel bad? (boys and girls)	✓	✓
* If a married daughter comes to stay with parents people don't force her to wear Sari. (boys and girls)	✓	✓
Category 3.3	1	6
* I am a modern girl and I like to wear and I would like to continue wearing all kinds of dresses. (a girl)	✓	✓
* *Bhabhi* is just like us. She used to wear such dresses before marriage, so why not now? (girls)	—	✓

(Contd.)

SITUATION 8 : *(Contd.)*

	Frequency	
	Before treat-ment	After treat-ment
* If I do not protest today, the tradition will continue and in future we will also have to suffer. (girls)	—	/

Choice 4

Any other alternative.	8	10
* I will explain to *Bhabhi* that she cannot have such demands immediately after marriage. First she should please the elders by doing housework and offering her services and then expect favours. (a boy)	/	—
* *Bhabhi* should be allowed to wear a gown while sleeping. (a girl)	/	/
* *Bhabhi* should be allowed to wear Salwar-Kameez but skirts do not look proper on a married woman. (boys and girls)	/	/
* *Bhabhi* should not wear dresses which would expose her body. (boys and girls)	/	/
* I will reason out with *Bhabhi* so that she does not feel bad; she is after all, new to the family. (a boy)	/	/
* A daughter-in-law should not cross limits in her dress. (boys and girls)	/	/
* *Bhabhi* or for that matter, any woman should not be allowed too much liberty. (a boy)	/	/
* I will explain to elders that Salwar-Kameez is a safer and more comfortable dress for working in the house. (a girl)	—	/

(Contd.)

SITUATION 8 : *(Contd.)*

	Frequency	
	Before treat-ment	After treat-ment
* A daughter-in-law cannot be allowed liberty in dressing which would invite adverse criticism from society. (boys and girls)	✓	✓

Observations

The response in general after treatment definitely shows change resulting into a more liberal outlook *vis-a-vis* dress code for married women as shown by the decreased number for Choice 1 and also for Choice 2 (of those who lack courage to stand up in support of their belief). The response in case of Choice 3 indicates marked change in favour of a liberal dress code for all women (frequency changed from 26 before treatment to 58 after treatment). The views given under Choice 4, however, show a mixture of conservative and change-prone views, but the number is much smaller than for Choice 3.

A remarkable point to note is that no respondent challenged the liberty of dress given to males (married or unmarried). Also it is quite apparent that the majority of respondents were not familiar with the variety of dresses accepted as social norms by different societies in different parts of India.

SITUATION 9

IX. A group of boys and girls in your class planned mischief against a new teacher but got caught. You are not in this group. The Principal gives very harsh punishment to the boys in the group but gives just a verbal scolding to the girls.

	Frequency	
	Before treatment	After treatment
Choice 1		
You do not agree with the Principal's action but since you are not part of the group you will keep quiet.	3	3
* I would have protested if I were a boy. I am a girl and girls did not get harsh punishment so why should I protest? (girls)	_/	_/
* I am not among those punished so why should I protest? (a boy and a girl)	_/	_/
* Girls are like our sisters. It is not proper to oppose any leniency extended to them. (a boy)	—	_/
Choice 2		
You will openly say that the action shows partiality and oppose it.	40	44
* If boys and girls are to be considered equal and are equally involved in mischief, punishment has to be equal. (boys and girls)	_/	_/
* I will go on strike till girls are given equal punishment. (a boy)	_/	_/
* I will go on fast till girls are given equal punishment. (a boy)	_/	_/
* Girls won't come to their senses if you simply scold them. (boys and girls)	_/	_/

(Contd.)

SITUATION 9 : *(Contd.)*

	Frequency	
	Before treat-ment	After treat-ment
* Girls are bold enough to take any harsh punishment. (girls)	_/	_/
* Girls want all the privileges of equality then why not equal punishment? (boys)	_/	_/
* Beating girls is not a sin. (girls)	—	_/
Choice 3		
You agree with the Principal's action.		
Category 3.1	8	3
* Boys can tolerate beating because their bodies are stronger. (boys and girls)	_/	_/
* If boys do not take the initiative girls never venture to play mischief. (girls)	_/	_/
* Scolding would have strong enough impact on girls but boys would behave badly again if you don't beat them. (boys and girls)	_/	—
* Boys are usually responsible for initiating mischief. (girls)	_/	—
* This is how it is done usually. (a boy)	_/	—
Category 3.2	1	0
* In no other field, girls are really given equal treatment. Why support equal treatment only when it comes to punishment? (girls)	_/	—

(Contd.)

SITUATION 9 : *(Contd.)*

	Frequency	
	Before treat-ment	After treat-ment
Choice 4		
Any other alternative.		
Category 4.1	—	1
* Girls can be given some other punishment if not beating. (a boy)		
Category 4.2	1	5
* It is not proper to beat girls. But even boys should not be beaten. Both should be scolded or given some other suitable punish-ment. (boys and girls)		

Observations

Here we may note that this is a school situation and not a family situation like other situations under discussion. Even before the treatment there was absence of gender bias with most of the respondents as can be judged from responses in case of Choice 2. There is emphasis on equality and radical egalitarianism rather than on equity, which has not been affected by the treatment. This is a relatively rare situation wherein boys are the victims of gender bias.

Choice 3, Category 3.2 is a response from a girl who is apparently disturbed at the superficial support to gender-equality.

Choice 4, Category 4.2 may be judged as a rational response of those accepting genuine gender-equality. The number of respondents after treatment has gone up to 5 from just 1 before treatment.

SITUATION 10

X. You are a member of a youth organization which decides to launch a crusade against social evils. A procession is planned to generate social awareness against dowry. The procession is going to pass through your neighbourhood. Your past experience has shown that if you participate in the procession your neighbours are going to ridicule you later. Many of them have taken dowry so it is quite likely that relations with them could get strained. Under the circumstances —

	Frequency	
	Before treatment	After treatment
Choice 1 To avoid any conflict with neighbours you will question the effectiveness of such an action and persuade your fellow members to cancel the procession.	3	1
* This programme will not achieve anything. (boys)		
Choice 2 You will participate in the procession.		
Category 2.1	20	18
* Because dowry is a very bad (gruesome) social evil. (boys and girls)	✓	✓
* Because dowry is a legal offence. (boys and girls)	—	✓
Category 2.2	1	4
* My father is very rich and he can afford to give me dowry but still I will join the procession. (a girl)	✓	✓
* People forget that if you take dowry today, you give double tomorrow. (a boy)	—	✓
* Even if my parents had demanded dowry in past, I will join the procession. (a boy)	✓	✓

(Contd.)

SITUATION 10 : *(Contd.)*

	Frequency	
	Before treatment	After treatment
* Neighbours may laugh today but tomorrow when they will have to give dowry, they will cry. (a boy)	—	✓
Category 2.3	24	27
* Not to participate in such programmes is an act of a traitor. (boys and girls)	—	✓
* One must make sacrifices for social reforms. (boys and girls)	✓	✓
* One has to be bold and not pay any attention to ridicule when you are fighting for a good cause. (boys and girls)	✓	✓
* One must fight on the side of justice and truth. (a boy)	✓	✓
* One must actively fight against social evils. (boys and girls)	✓	✓
* If youth of India won't fight against dowry, who would? (boys and girls)	✓	✓
* I believe in action and not just lip-sympathy. (a boy)	✓	✓
* We must go ahead and fight for what we believe in. (boys and girls)	✓	✓
Category 2.4	2	7
* I will not only join the procession but convince my critics of its benefits. (a boy)	✓	✓
* I will join and bring my neighbours also to join. (boys and girls)	✓	✓

(Contd.)

SITUATION 10 : *(Contd.)*

	Frequency	
	Before treatment	After treatment
* My neighbours should also realise that I belong to the new generation. (a boy)	—	✓
* I will join and also make efforts to create public awareness. (boys and girls)	—	✓
Category 2.4	5	7
* Unless dowry is abolished, girls will not be happy. (girls)	✓	✓
* Women are burnt alive because of dowry. (boys and girls)	✓	✓
Category 2.5	1	0
* I will protest because in our caste they demand dowry. (a girl)	✓	—
Choice 3 You will not try to cancel the procession but will find an excuse at the last minute to slip away from the procession.	2	2
* I am worried about facing ridicule. (a boy and a girl)	✓	✓
* I do not want my neighbours to look down upon me. (a boy and a girl)	✓	✓

Observations

Apparently the word "dowry" has influenced the response even before the treatment. Most of the respondents were against dowry from the beginning. This fact probably explains the statistical test showing no significant change. After treatment, however, there is a sharp increase of those who were prepared to act for the cause (Choice 2, particularly Categories 2.2 and 2.3).

SITUATION 11

XI. In Mumbai, they run special "Women's Trains" at the time when most offices finish work. There is a proposal for "Women's Buses" on similar lines in your city. The decision about the proposal will be taken by referendum. In your family there is no working women.

	Frequency	
	Before treat-ment	After treat-ment
Choice 1		
You will vote for "women's buses".		
Category 1.1	9	15
* Women have to go home and cook. (boys and girls)	/	/
* Women have to rush to job and then rush back home to shoulder other responsibilities and they get tired. (boys and girls)	/	/
* Women work for a better life for their families. (boys and girls)	/	/
* Women work as much as men do. (girls)	/	/
* Women deserve as much respect as men do. (girls)	/	/
Category 1.2	2	10
* I am a girl and I would like to work in future. (a girl)	/	/
* If today we show concern about somebody's problems, tomorrow someone will understand our problems. (boys and girls)	—	/
* Tomorrow we may also face this issue. (a girl)	—	/

SITUATION 11 : *(Contd.)*

	Frequency	
	Before treatment	After treatment
Category 1.3	5	11
* If someone benefits from our support, we should offer support. (boys and girls)	—	√
* Even if no woman from our family works, we should think about others. (boys)	√	√
* This will encourage more women to work. (girls)	—	√
* The whole world is our family. (a boy)	—	√
Category 1.4	16	35
* Women have to face eveteasing. (boys and girls)	√	√
* I won't like any man evetease my sister. (a boy)	√	—
* Women find it difficult to catch train with men pushing around. (boys and girls)	√	√
* Women may die if accidentally pushed out of train. (a boy)	—	√
* Separate train will be convenient because women can travel without any tensions. (boys and girls)	√	√
* Today because of impact of films and television you find 'road-romeos' everywhere. (boys and girls)	√	√
* There is a risk of purse or jewellery getting stolen. (boys and girls)	√	√
Category 1.5	1	1
* Because such trains have proven successful in Mumbai. (a boy)	√	√

(Contd.)

SITUATION 11 : *(Contd.)*

	Frequency	
	Before treat-ment	After treat-ment
Choice 2		
You will vote against "women's buses".		
Category 2.1	3	0
* We will not permit girls to work. (boys)	/	—
* It is our Indian tradition that girls should not work outside home. (boys)	/	—
Category 2.2	2	2
* Everyone should get equal benefits. (a boy)	/	/
* More number of men work compared to women. (a boy)	/	/
Category 2.3	0	2
* Women show better awareness and they can protect themselves. They do not need any such help. (girls)	—	/
Choice 3		
You will not vote.	2	1
* Voting is not going to benefit us in any way. (boys)		
Choice 4		
Any other alternative.	3	3
* I would propose that you have separate "Men's Trains" also because these days men and women are equal. (girls)	/	/
* Men also face difficulties in catching trains/buses. (boys and girls)	—	/

Observations

Even before the treatment there were only a few (only five boys) who were against the proposal for starting a Women's Bus, but many were apathetic about it. After treatment many more boys and girls were in favour of the proposal and their reasoning was based on equity. Another interesting point was that some girls appreciated that men also faced similar difficulties (Choice 4). There is a good feature showing influence of the treatment (Choice 2, Category 2.1); here the die-hard gender-bias existing before the treatment is not seen after the treatment. Thus a positive trend in favour of gender equity is seen though statistically the change is not significant (Table 4.22).

SITUATION 12

XII. You support gender equality and therefore you frequently become victim of jabs and ridicule. Sometimes you have to face strong opposition in your family and peer group and at times you also get scolded for advocating gender equality.

	Frequency	
	Before treat-ment	After treat-ment
Choice 1 You will change your stand on gender equality because it creates problems for you.	0	2
* Sometimes you have to change. You cannot obstinately hold to your views all the time. (a girl)	—	_/
* You may have to change your views based on your experiences. (a girl)	—	_/
Choice 2 You will stick to your views but will not let them be reflected in your public behaviour.	4	2
* I won't like people ridiculing me. (a boy)	_/	_/
* I would end up quarrelling if someone would pass an adverse comment. (a boy)	_/	—
* I won't like people adversely commenting upon my ideas. (a boy)	_/	—
* I am scared of facing opposition from friends and family. (a girl)	_/	—

SITUATION 12 : *(Contd.)*

	Frequency	
	Before treat-ment	After treat-ment
Choice 3		
You will stick to your stand and continue to think and behave the way you do now.		
Category 3.1	13	30
* I am a staunch believer in equality of sexes. (boys and girls)	/	/
* I am confident that if not today, in future people will believe in equality. (boys and girls)	/	/
* Only gender equality can help women. (girls)	/	/
* The number of people believing in gender equality is on the rise. (boys and girls)	—	/
* Government also supports gender equality. (a boy)	—	/
* My values are appropriate to time and are also just. (a boy)	/	/
Category 3.2	13	19
* To pay attention to ridicule and comments is a sign of stupidity and cowardice. (girls)	—	/
* Gradually I will turn my opponents into supporters. (boys)	/	/
* Your action should match your ideas. (a boy)	/	/
* If you take a stand you should be ready to face all odds. (boys and girls)	/	/

(Contd.)

SITUATION 12 : *(Contd.)*

	Frequency	
	Before treatment	After treatment
* I believe that God is on the side of truth — I will stick to truth and fight injustice without being daunted by any odds. (a boy)	—	✓
* People who ridicule the idea today may suffer tomorrow and then they will realize.	—	✓
* I don't usually change my views as I am very firm temperamentally. (a girl)	—	✓
* From my childhood I have confidence in myself; if my opinion is right, I do not give it up. (a boy)	—	✓
* If you create public awareness people will automatically stop making fun of the issue and activists. (boys and girls)	—	✓
Category 3.3	1	8
* Only when more and more people will believe in gender equality, our country/society will progress. (boys and girls)	✓	✓
* Our country is independent and we have freedom of thought. (a boy)	—	✓
* We want our country to be at par with other countries. (boys and girls)	—	✓

Choice 4

Any other alternative.

Category 4.1	0	1
* I will stick to my stand but I will not impose it on anyone else. (a girl)	—	✓
Category 4.2	2	0
* Men and women are not equal so the question does not arise. (boys)	✓	—

Observations

After treatment, as responses to Choice 3 indicate, the number of respondents supporting gender equality and ready to act accordingly increased to a remarkable extent, but as the categories of responses show, for different reasons. In Choice 4, the response under Category 4.2 deserves our notice. Here two staunch holders of gender-bias did not take the same stand after treatment.

GENERAL OBSERVATIONS BASED ON QUALITATIVE ANALYSIS OF JUSTIFICATIONS

(1) It was interesting to see the wide range of justifications given by students in support of the same choice (e.g. reasons given for various categories of choices) on the twelve situations on value-test.

(2) When asked to give reason for a choice many students just repeated the option instead of giving a reason for selecting it, or gave a totally irrelevant statement.

(3) Overall command over language and expression of ideas was found to be poor. Many students lacked the skill for choice of proper words and clarity was low in their answers.

(4) Justifications/Reasons given in the posttest showed more cases of multiple arguments to support a choice of option showing that many aspects of a situation were considered while forming opinion or making value judgement which may be considered a positive influence of treatment.

(5) Even many girls have strong gender bias, which in many cases is unfavourable for females.

INFLUENCE OF INDEPENDENT VARIABLES

One of the objectives of the present study was to study influence of sex of the subject, education of mother, education of father, profession of mother, profession of father and type of family on effectiveness of Value Discussion Model in terms of change in attitude towards gender equality, gender-stereotyping and value judgement. Results of ANCOVA are presented in Tables 4.23 to 4.40.

Comparison of Adjusted Mean Attitude towards Gender-Equality of Males and Females

Adjusted mean attitudes towards Gender-Equality of males and females was compared by considering pretest scores of the same variable as co-variate. The data were analysed through ANCOVA and results are given in Table 4.23.

TABLE 4.23: Summary of ANCOVA for Attitude towards Gender-Equality taking Sex as Source of Variance

Source of Variance	df	SSy.x	MSSy.x	Fy.x
Sex	1	1107.808	1107.808	1.312
Error	55	46448.251	844.514	

In Table 4.23 the adjusted F-value is not significant at 0.05 level.It may therefore be concluded that sex of the student had no significant influence on the effect of treatment in case of attitude towards gender equality.

Comparison of Adjusted Mean Gender-Stereotyping by Males and Females

Comparison of adjusted mean gender-stereotyping of males and females was done considering pretest scores of the same variable as co-variate. The results of ANCOVA are summarised in Table 4.24.

In Table 4.24 the adjusted F-value is not significant at 0.05 level. Thus, the null hypothesis (No. 8) that the adjusted mean-gender-stereotype scores of males and females will not differ significantly is not rejected.

TABLE 4.24 : Summary of ANCOVA for Gender-Stereotyping taking Sex as a Source of Variance

Source of Variance	df	SSy.x	MSSy.x	Fy.x
Sex	1	4.007	4.007	0.346
Error	32	370.788	11.587	

It may therefore be concluded that sex of the student did not significantly influence the effect of treatment with respect to gender-stereotyping.

Comparison of Adjusted Mean Value Judgement of Males and Females

Adjusted mean value judgement of males and females was compared considering pretest scores of the same variable as co-variate. Table 4.25 summarizes the results of ANCOVA.

TABLE 4.25 : Summary of ANCOVA for Value-Judgement taking Sex as a Source of Variance

Source of Variance:	df	SSy.x	MSSy.x	Fy.x
Sex	1	1.683	1.683	0.096
Error	55	963.74	17.523	

In Table 4.25 the adjusted F-value is not significant at 0.05 level. It may therefore be concluded that sex of the students had no significant influence on the effect of treatment with respect to value judgement.

Comparison of Adjusted Mean Attitude towards Gender Equality of Children of Housewives and of Employed Mothers

The comparison of adjusted mean-attitude towards gender-equality of children of housewives and those of employed mothers was carried out considering pretest scores of the same variable as co-variate. The data were analysed through ANCOVA and results are given in Table 4.26.

TABLE 4.26 : Summary of ANCOVA for Attitude towards Gender-Equality taking Mother's Profession as a Source of Variance

Source of Variance	df	SSy.x	MSSy.x	Fy.x
Mother's Profession	1	754.83.	754.83	0.887
Error	55	46801.177	850.930	

In Table 4.26, the adjusted F-value is not significant at 0.05 level. It may therefore be concluded that mother's profession did not significantly influence the effect of treatment in case of attitude towards gender equality.

Comparison of Adjusted Mean Gender-Stereotyping by Children of Housewives and of Employed Mothers

Adjusted mean-gender stereotyping of children of housewives and those of employed mothers was compared considering pretest scores of the same variable as covariate. The results of ANCOVA are presented in Table 4.27.

TABLE 4.27: Summary of ANCOVA for Gender-Stereotype taking Mother's Profession as Source of Variance

Source of Variance	df	SSy.x	MSSy.x	Fy.x
Mother's Profession	1	7.177	7.177	0.625
Error	32	367.619	11.488	

In Table 4.27 the adjusted F-value is not significant at 0.05 level. It may therefore be concluded that mother's profession did not have significant influence on the effect of treatment with respect to gender stereotyping.

Comparison of Adjusted Mean Value Judgement of Children of Housewives and of Employed Mothers

Adjusted mean value judgement of children of housewives and those of employed mothers were compared considering pretest scores of the same variable as co-variate. Table 4.28 summarises the results of ANCOVA.

TABLE 4.28: Summary of ANCOVA for Value Judgement taking Mother's Profession as a Source of Variance

Source of Variance	df	SSy.x	MSSy.x	Fy.x
Mother's Profession	1	0.169	0.169	0.010
Error	55	965.257	17.550	

In Table 4.28 the adjusted F-value is not significant at 0.05 level. It may therefore be concluded that mother's profession did not significantly influence the effect of treatment with respect to value judgement.

Comparison of Adjusted Mean Attitude towards Gender Equality of Students whose Fathers belong to Different Professional Categories

One of the objectives was to compare adjusted mean attitude towards gender equality of students whose fathers belonged to three different professional categories; namely, Labour; Farming and Business; White Collar Jobs and Professionals. Comparison was made considering pre-test scores of the same variables as co-variate. The data were analysed through ANCOVA and results are given in Table 4.29.

TABLE 4.29 : Summary of ANCOVA for Attitude towards Gender Equality taking Father's Profession as a Source of Variance

Source of Variance	df	SSy.x	MSSy.x	Fy.x
Father's Profession	2	5637.447	2818.723	3.564*
Error	53	41917.991	790.905	

*Significant at 0.05 level.

In Table 4.29 the adjusted F-value is significant at 0.05 level. It may therefore be concluded that father's profession had significant influence on the effect of treatment with respect to attitude towards gender equality.

Comparison of Adjusted Mean Gender-Stereotyping by Students whose Fathers belong to Different Professional Categories

Comparison of adjusted mean gender-stereotyping by students whose fathers belonged to three different professional categories, namely Labour; Farming and Business; White Collar Jobs and Professionals, was made considering pretest score of the same variables as co-variate. The results of ANCOVA are summarized in Table 4.30.

TABLE 4.30 : Summary of ANCOVA for Gender-Stereotyping taking Father's Profession as a Source of Variance

Source of Variance	df	SSy.x	MSSy.x	Fy.x
Father's Profession	2	52.377	26.189	2.518
Error	31	322.418	10.401	

In Table 4.30 it can be seen that adjusted F-value is not significant at 0.05 level. It may therefore be concluded that father's profession did not have significant influence on effect of treatment with respect to gender stereotyping.

Comparison of Adjusted Mean Value Judgement of Students whose Fathers belong to Different Professional Categories

Adjusted mean value judgement of students whose fathers belonged to different professional categories, namely Labour; Farming and Business; White Collar Jobs and Professionals, were compared considering pretest scores of the same variable as co-variate. Table 4.31 summarizes the results of ANCOVA.

TABLE 4.31: Summary of ANCOVA for Value Judgement taking Father's Profession as a Source of Variance

Source of Variance	df	SSy.x	MSSy.x	Fy.x
Father's Profession	2	4.578	2.289	0.127
Error	53	954.737	18.014	

In Table 4.31 the adjusted F-value is not significant at 0.05 level. It may therefore be concluded that father's profession did not have significant influence on effect of treatment with respect to value judgement.

Comparison of Adjusted Mean Attitude towards Gender-Equality of Students whose Mothers have Different Levels of Education

Comparison of adjusted mean attitude towards gender equality of students whose mothers had different levels of education (0 to Std.7; Std. 8 to SSC and College education) was made considering pretest scores on the same variables as covariate. The results of ANCOVA are shown in Table 4.32.

TABLE 4.32: Summary of ANCOVA for Attitude towards Gender-Equality taking Mother's Education as a Source of Variance

Source of Variance	df	SSy.x	MSSy.x	Fy.x
Mother's Education	2	1122.019	561.009	0.652
Error	54	46434.040	859.890	

In Table 4.32 the adjusted F-value is not significant at 0.05 level.It may therefore be concluded that mother's education did not significantly influence effect of treatment with respect to attitude towards gender equality.

Comparison of Adjusted Mean Gender-Stereotyping by Students whose Mothers have Different Levels of Education

Adjusted mean gender-stereotyping by students whose mothers had different levels of education (0 to Std.7; Std.8 to SSC and College education) was compared considering the pretest scores of the same variable as co-variate. The data were analysed through ANCOVA and results are given in Table 4.33.

TABLE 4.33 : Summary of ANCOVA for Gender Stereotype taking Mother's Education as a Source of Variance

Source of Variance	df	SSy.x	MSSy.x	Fy.x
Mother's Education	2	64.303	32.152	3.210
Error	31	310.492	10.016	

In Table 4.33 the adjusted *t*-value is not significant at 0.05 level. It may therefore be concluded that mother's education had no significant influence on the effect of treatment in case of gender stereotyping.

Comparison of Adjusted Mean Value Judgement of Students whose Mothers had Different Levels of Education

Adjusted mean value judgement of students whose mothers had different levels of education (0 to Std.7; Std.8 to SSC and College education) was compared considering pretest scores of the same variables as co-variate. Table 4.34 summarizes the results of ANCOVA.

TABLE 4.34 : Summary of ANCOVA for Value Judgement taking Mother's Education as a Source of Variance

Source of Variance	df	SSy.x	MSSy.x	Fy.x
Mother's Education	2	7.305	3.652	0.206
Error	54	958.121	17.743	

Table 4.34 shows that the adjusted F-value is not significant at 0.05 level. It may therefore be concluded that mother's education did not have significant influence on the effect of treatment in case of value judgement.

Comparison of Adjusted Mean Attitude towards Gender Equality of Students whose Fathers had Different Levels of Education

Adjusted mean attitude towards gender equality of students whose fathers had different levels of education (school education and college education) was compared considering pretest scores on the same variable as co-variate. The results of ANCOVA are shown in Table 4.35.

TABLE 4.35 : Summary of ANCOVA for Attitude toward Gender Equality taking Father's Education as a Source of Variance

Source of Variance	df	SSy.x	MSSy.x	Fy.x
Father's Education	1	515.713	515.713	0.603
Error	55	47040.346	855.279	

Table 4.35 shows that the adjusted F-value is not significant at 0.05 level. It may therefore be concluded that father's education did not significantly influence the effect of treatment with respect to attitude towards gender equality.

Comparison of Adjusted Mean Gender-Stereotyping by Students whose Fathers had Different Levels of Education

Comparison of adjusted mean gender stereotype of students whose fathers had different levels of education (school education and college education) was made considering pretest scores of the same variables as co-variate. Table 4.36 shows the results of ANCOVA.

TABLE 4.36 : Summary of ANCOVA for Gender Stereotype taking Father's Education as a Source of variance

Source of Variance	df	SSy.x	MSSy.x	Fy.x
Father's Education	1	0.003	0.003	0.000
Error	32	374.792	11.712	

In Table 4.36 the adjusted F-value is not significant at 0.05 level.It may therefore be concluded that father's education did not have significant influence on effect of treatment with respect to gender stereotype.

Comparison of Adjusted Mean Value Judgement of Students whose Fathers had Different Levels of Education

Comparison of adjusted mean value judgement of students whose fathers had different levels of education (school education and college education) was made considering pretest scores of the same variable as co-variate. The data were analysed through ANCOVA and results are shown in Table 4.37.

TABLE 4.37 : Summary of ANCOVA for Value Judgement taking Father's Education as a Source of Variance

Source of Variance	df	SSy.x	MSSy.x	Fy.x
Father's Education	1	0.016	0.016	0.001
Error	55	965.409	17.553	

Table 4.37 shows that the adjusted F-value is not significant at 0.05 level. It may therefore be concluded that father's education did not have significant influence on the effect of treatment in case of value judgement.

Comparison of Adjusted Mean Attitude towards Gender-Equality of Students from Joint Families and those from Nuclear Families

Adjusted mean attitude towards gender-equality of students from joint families and those from nuclear families was compared by considering pretest scores of the same variable as co-variate and data were analysed through ANCOVA. The results of ANCOVA are given in Table 4.38.

TABLE 4.38: Summary of ANCOVA for Attitude towards Gender-Equality taking Type of Family as a Source of Variance

Source of Variance	df	SSy.x	MSSy.x	Fy.x
Type of Family	1	250.875	250.875	0.323
Error	53	41167.368	776.743	

In Table 4.38 the adjusted F-value is not significant at 0.05 level. It may therefore be concluded that type of family did not have significant influence on the effect of treatment with respect to attitude towards gender-equality.

Comparison of Adjusted Mean Gender-Stereotyping by Students from Joint Families and those from Nuclear Families

Comparison of adjusted mean gender stereotype of students from joint families and those from nuclear families was made considering pretest scores of the same variables as co-variate. The results of ANCOVA are summarized in Table 4.39.

TABLE 4.39: Summary of ANCOVA for Gender Stereotyping taking Type of Family as a Source of Variance

Source of Variance	df	SSy.x	MSSy.x	Fy.x
Type of Family	1	0.364	0.364	0.030
Error	30	366.157	12.205	

Table 4.39 shows that the adjusted F-value is not significant at 0.05 level. It may therefore be concluded that type of family did not significantly influence the effect of treatment in case of gender-stereotyping.

Comparison of Adjusted Mean Value Judgement of Students from Joint Families and those from Nuclear Families

Adjusted mean value judgement of students from joint families and those from nuclear families was compared by considering pretest scores of the same variables as co-variate. Table 4.40 summarizes the results of ANCOVA.

TABLE 4.40 : Summary of ANCOVA for Value Judgement taking Type of Family as a Source of Variance

Source of Variance	df	SSy.x	MSSy.x	Fy.x
Type of Family	1	32.654	32.654	1.889
Error	53	916.171	17.286	

In Table 4.40 the adjusted F-value is not significant at 0.05 level. It may therefore be concluded that type of family did not have significant influence on the effect of treatment with respect to value judgement.

To find out the opinion of participating students about the programme, the experimental group was asked to opine whether the programme was interesting and useful. Students were also encouraged to write comments. Table 4.41 summarizes students' opinions about the programme.

TABLE 4.41 : Students' Opinions about the Value Discussion Approach in Communication for Gender Equality

	Opinion	Percentage
1.	Interesting	1.8
2.	Interesting and Useful	80.7
3.	Useful	5.3
4.	Useful but Not Interesting	1.8
5.	No Answer	10.5
		100.0

QUALITATIVE OBSERVATIONS DURING THE EXPERIMENT

Gender is one of the most significant characteristics that we use for identifying an individual. Segregation by gender is a widespread norm in Indian society, be it at family functions, weddings, religious places of worship, ceremonies, sitting arrangement or pattern in schools, colleges, meetings, or in public transport.

The school to which the experimental group belonged was no different. As one entered the main gate of the building, two staircases on opposite sides led to the first floor — one marked "For Boys" and the other "For Girls". In every class, boys and girls sat in distinctly separate sections. In recess they ate snacks, talked or played with only the students of the same sex. Whatever interactions took place between boys and girls were to a large extent limited to making sly remarks or arguing.

(1) When during the pretesting the students were responding to the self-administered questionnaire on background information, many got stuck when they came to the item "mother's profession". They were doubtful if household work could be considered a valid response. Many wrote "nothing" or "no profession" when

the mother was a housewife.

(2) On the day of the first dilemma session, girls and boys were simply not willing to sit on the same bench nor in the seats next to one another. They refused to be part of the same small-groups even if their choice of option required it. They also avoided addressing a student of the opposite sex directly. The investigator had to resort to all kinds of techniques from requesting, coaxing and challenging to forcing to begin interaction between boys and girls.

A marked change in this tendency was observed as the sessions progressed. The change was gradual and slow. When the discussion got heated and the involvement of the students was at the peak, they seemed to forget temporarily the gender difference, asked questions directly and demanded answers.

(3) Very few boys and girls (only two girls and one boy in the first four sessions) were ready on their own to come forward as group monitors to present the arguments constructed by their respective small groups. The number went up to about 10 students after much persuasion. More girls than boys were willing to come forward for presentation.

(4) There was a bunch of six boys who were always up to mischief. They tried to disrupt the flow of discussion by passing comments, teasing the girls, testing the investigator's patience by asking irrelevant questions, or frequently changing groups mid-way. When asked to put down their response on a piece of paper, they signed it with names like 'Khalnayak', 'Gumnam", 'Benam Badshah' and '420' clearly showing influence of commercial cinema and television. This influence was also reflected in the way they framed arguments, and gave examples (e.g. changing the surname :

Divya Bharti → Divya Nadiadwala

Sharmila Tagore → Sharmila Pataudi

(5) Throughout the sessions, girls participated with more serious interest and involvement. Many boys had a rather casual attitude to the exercise and a few did not try to hide their feeling that if it were not compulsory to participate in the discussion, they would rather not. Boys and girls received the dilemma presentation with equal attention and interest but girls gave more serious thought

to the discussion. Girls also showed better command over written and spoken language while making presentation and participating in discussion and had better style of expression.

(6) Girls showed interest in the issues beyond the dilemma sessions and sought out more information during recess or before and after the formal session. They narrated their personal experiences, raised doubts and expressed their eagerness for more sessions. Girls also tried to establish personal rapport with the investigator asking her personal questions about her family, marriage and work and complimenting her on a new dress or hairstyle.

They came forward with support and sympathy when some of the boys tried their best to disrupt the sessions. A significant reason could be that the investigator was of the same gender.

(7) The language used by boys and girls is full of cliches, e.g. *Stri lagna kareene saat feraa-na atut bandhan-maa bandhaai jaay chhe* (On marriage, a woman becomes honour-bound to observe vows of marriage which is indissoluble),

or

Baalak-naa janm pacchi stri patni mati jai maa-nu mamtaabharyun mahaan roop dhaaran kare chhe (On attainment of motherhood a woman gets transformed from the role of wife into the noble role of a loving mother),

or

Haji aapano samaaj jive chhe. Mari nathi gayo (Our society is still alive and kicking, not dead),

or

Chhokri aakhare paarku dhan chhe (A daughter really belongs to someone else — meaning 'Parents are only temporary custodians of a daughter'),

or

Ghar-to stri-thi-j shobhe. (It is only the woman who adorns the home).

(8) Excerpts recorded from Hindi commercial films seemed to be the mode of presentation attracting maximum attention and sustained interest, followed by skits presented by guest artists. When a film clip from 'Aandhi' was shown and students saw Sanjeev Kumar on screen, the murmurs of recognition were heard all over. Amitabh Bachchan in 'Abhiman' was greeted with loud

claps. Both the clips were viewed in total silence and rapt attention. Role-plays presented by students themselves attracted attention but performers tended to be self-conscious and it gave the mischief-makers an opportunity for cat-calls and passing comments on their class-mates. When a dilemma was presented using puppets, it attracted attention but at times students seemed to get more engrossed in the movements of puppets which they found amusing. This could temporarily shift students' attention from the content.

Using the VCR and TV, however, was the most cumbersome exercise for the investigator. For a film clip lasting for two or three minutes, it took more than an hour to take out the TV and VCR from a locked cupboard, transporting them to the classroom or transporting almost sixty students to another room where TV/VCR could be placed. Connections and setting also took time and after all the pains taken by the principal, class teacher and peons, the final outcome could be jeopardised by sudden electricity failure.

(9) Apart from the strength of dilemma and presentation several other incidental factors affected the discussion and final outcome. If the investigator was given an hour just before the recess, students made it a point to ensure that the session got over before recess. When the recess bell went, many did not want to stay back to cast their vote for the final choice. On the other hand if the session preceded a class when either the teacher or the subject was not their favourite, students tried to keep a relaxed pace of discussion and took time to vote trying to see that the session spilled over to the other class. Some of them offered to make a special request to the concerned teacher to sacrifice his or her class for this 'important' project. Similarly, the investigator was not quite welcome if the hour allotted to her fell during Drawing or Physical Education (sports) class. She was received with great enthusiasm otherwise.

(10) Space was the biggest constraint. No large and uncluttered room was available where small groups could form circles and work at some distance from one another. All the grouping, re-grouping and small-group discussions had to be organised in a small classroom, cluttered from wall to wall with benches. Construction work going on in the adjoining building forced everyone, including

the investigator to shout and heavy traffic in the busy streets and the nearby market-place was a constant backdrop.

(11) After about ten to twelve sessions the whole approach of Value Discussion became very predictable for students. Unless the dilemma was strong and presented in a very attractive mode, some students started showing signs of losing interest and complaining of monotony.

(12) An incident during the experiment period demonstrates how informal socialization in the school reinforces gender bias.

In one of the discussion sessions (following viewing of the excerpt of Hindi film 'Abhiman' on video) some of the boys (the usual mischief-makers) started creating a lot of disturbance. They wanted to go and play volleyball. The disruption affected other students and as a last resort, the investigator had to call their class-teacher (who had the reputation of being strict, and was one of the few teachers who commanded respect from students) and also the school Principal. They came and reprimanded the mischief-makers. At the end of reproof they tried to motivate boys saying "You should be ashamed that girls are getting so much ahead of you in everything. Have you ever given it a thought that if this continues, in not so far away future, they will be occupying all the important posts and you boys will be relegated to kitchen (*Saansi pakadwaano vakhat aavshe, moorkhaao!*)".

5

RESULTS AND DISCUSSION

The major results of the study are discussed in the present chapter. The chapter also presents conclusion and recommendations arrived at through the study.

THE FINAL POSITION ON NULL HYPOTHESES

The final position on the Null Hypotheses with respect to the objectives of the study is given in Table 5.1.

TABLE 5.1: Position with respect to Null Hypothesis at the End of the Investigation

Change in Objectives	*Conclusion*	*Null Hypothesis about the hypothesis*
Objective 1 : *To Study the Effectiveness of Value-Discussion Model in Terms of Change in (1.1, 1.2 and 1.3)*		
1.1 Attitude towards gender equality	There will be no significant difference between adjusted mean-attitude-towards-gender-equality scores of the control group and those of the experimental group. Or There will be no significant difference between the pretest	Retained

TABLE 5.1 (*Contd.*)

Change in Objectives	*Null Hypothesis*	*Conclusion about the hypothesis*
	and posttest scores of attitude towards gender equality in the experimental group.	Retained
	Or	
1.2 Gender-stereo-typing	There will be no significant difference between adjusted mean gender-stereotype scores of the control group and those of the experimental group.	Rejected
	Or	
	There will be no significant difference between the pretest and posttest gender-stereotype scores in the experimental group.	Rejected
1.3 Value-Judgement	There will be no significant difference between adjusted mean value-judgement scores of the control group and those of the experimental group.	Rejected
	Or	
	There will be no significant difference between the pretest and posttest value-judgement scores in the experimental group.	Rejected

Objective 2 : To Study the Influence of the following Variables on Effectiveness of Value-Discussion —

(*Contd.*)

TABLE 5.1 : *(Contd.)*

Variable	*Null Hypothesis*	*Conclusion about the hypothesis*
2.1 Sex of the subject	There will be no significant difference in the adjusted mean attitude-towards-gender-equality scores of males and females in the experimental groups.	Retained
	There will be no significant difference in the adjusted mean-gender-stereotype scores of males and females in the experimental group.	Retained
	Or There will be no significant difference in the adjusted mean-value-judgement scores of males and females in the experimental group.	Retained
2.2 Profession of mother	There will be no significant difference between adjusted mean-attitude-towards-gender-equality scores of children of housewives and those of working mothers in the experimental group.	Retained
	Or There will be no significant difference between adjusted mean-gender-stereotype scores of children of housewives and those of working mothers in the experimental group.	Retained
	Or There will be no significant difference between adjusted mean value-judgement scores of children of housewives and those of working mothers in the experimental group.	Retained

(Contd.)

TABLE 5.1 : *(Contd.)*

Variable	*Null Hypothesis*	*Conclusion about the hypothesis*
2.3 Profession of father	There will be no significant difference between adjusted mean-attitude-towards-gender-equality scores of students whose fathers belong to different professional categories in the experimental group.	Rejected
	Or	
	There will be no significant difference between adjusted mean-gender-stereotype scores of students whose fathers belong to different professional categories in the experimental group.	Retained
	Or	
	There will be no significant difference between adjusted mean-value-judgement scores of students whose fathers belong to different professional categories in the experimental group.	Retained
2.4 Education of mother	There will be no significant difference between adjusted mean-attitude-towards-gender-equality scores of students whose mothers had different levels of education in the experimental group.	Retained
	Or	
	There will be no significant difference between adjusted mean-gender-stereotype scores of students whose mothers had different levels of education in the experimental group.	Retained

(Contd.)

TABLE 5.1 : *(Contd.)*

Variable	*Null Hypothesis*	*Conclusion about the hypothesis*
	Or	
	There will be no significant difference between adjusted mean-value-judgement scores of students whose mothers had different levels of education in the experimental group.	Retained
2.5 Education of father	There will be no significant difference between adjusted mean-attitude-towards-gender-equality scores of students whose fathers had different levels of education in the experimental group.	Retained
	Or	
	There will be no significant difference between adjusted mean-gender-stereotype scores of students whose fathers had different levels of education in the experimental group.	Retained
	Or	
	There will be no significant difference between adjusted mean-value-judgement scores of students whose fathers had different levels of education in the experimental group.	Retained
2.6 Type of family	There will be no significant difference between adjusted mean-attitude-gender-equality scores of students from joint families and those from nuclear families in the experimental group.	Retained

(Contd.)

TABLE 5.1 : *(Contd.)*

Variable	*Null Hypothesis*	*Conclusion about the hypothesis*
	Or	
	There will be no significant difference between adjusted mean-gender-stereotype scores of students from joint families and those from nuclear families in the experimental group.	Retained
	Or	
	There will be no significant difference between adjusted mean-value-judgement scores of students from joint families and those from nuclear families in the experimental group.	Retained

Note : Value Clarification was evaluated through qualitative observation (Chapter 4)

SALIENT OUTCOMES

The quasi-experimental approach with pretest-posttest non-equivalent group design yielded the following major findings:

1. The Value Discussion Model did not significantly affect attitude towards gender equality (Tables 4.1 and 4.2).
2. The Value Discussion Model had significant positive effect on gender-stereotyping with respect to professions (Tables 4.3 and 4.4).
3. Professions considered appropriate for both genders before treatment remained in the same category after treatment (Table 4.7).
4. Before treatment professions of dancer, typist and social worker were considered appropriate for both genders but with slight

feminine inclination. After treatment, gender-stereotyping was reduced to some extent in case of social worker while the effect was negligible on professions of dancer and typist (Table 4.8).

5. Out of 13 professions considered appropriate for both genders but with slight masculine inclination before treatment, reduction in gender-stereotyping to some extent was observed after treatment in nine professions whereas the effect of treatment was negligible in case of four professions (Table 4.9).
6. Before treatment fashion modelling and dress designing were considered as professions more appropriate for women. After the treatment through Value Discussion Model, noteworthy reduction in gender stereotyping was found in both the professions (Table 4.10).
7. Before treatment the professions of chef, shopkeeper, electrician, collector, industrialist, manager and architect were considered more appropriate for men. After treatment noteworthy reduction in gender-stereotyping was observed in case of collector; gender-stereotyping was reduced up to some extent in case of shopkeeper, industrialist, manager and architect; while negligible change was observed in case of chef and electrician (Table 4.11).
8. Before treatment baby-sitting, nursing, housework and pre-school teaching were considered predominantly feminine professions. Noteworthy reduction in gender-stereotyping was observed after treatment in case of housework, while reduction to some extent was observed for baby sitting, nursing and pre-school teaching (Table 4.12).
9. Before treatment taxi-driver, farmer, waiter, mechanic and pilot were the five professions considered predominantly masculine. After treatment noteworthy reduction in gender-stereotyping was observed in case of waiter and pilot and reduction to some extent in taxi-driver and farmer. Negligible change was observed in case of mechanic (Table 4.13).
10. Out of the eight broad categories of reasons extended for considering a profession appropriate for only one gender, the following four categories were the most frequently cited before and after treatment : Knowledge, Skill and Art; Tradition/ Convention; Social Reasons; and Innate Qualities (for details

of categories please refer to pp. 76-81).

11. The maximum difference in frequencies before and after treatment was observed for the reason category 'Knowledge, Skill and Art'. Compared to this the difference observed for the categories 'Tradition/Convention' and 'Social Reasons' were lower. The difference was the least for the category 'Innate Qualities' (Table 4.18).
12. The Value Discussion Model had significant positive effect on value judgement with respect to gender equality (Tables 4.19 and 4.20).
13. Sex of the student had no significant influence on the effect of treatment with respect to attitude towards gender equality, gender-stereotyping and value judgement (Tables 4.23 to 4.25).
14. Profession of mother did not significantly influence the effect of treatment in case of attitude towards gender equality, gender-stereotyping and value judgement (Tables 4.26 to 4.28).
15. Profession of father had significant influence on the effect of treatment with respect to attitude towards gender equality (Table 4.29). Profession of father, however, did not have significant influence on the effect of treatment in case of gender-stereotyping or value judgement (Tables 4.30 and 4.31).
16. Education of mother did not significantly influence the effect of treatment with respect to attitude towards gender equality, gender-stereotyping and value judgement (Tables 4.32 to 4.34).
17. Education of father had no significant influence on the effect of treatment with respect to attitude towards gender equality, gender-stereotyping and value judgement (Tables 4.35 to 4.37).
18. Type of family did not significantly influence the effect of treatment with respect to attitude towards gender equality, gender-stereotyping and value judgement (Tables 4.38 to 4.40).

INTERPRETATION AND DISCUSSION OF THE FINDINGS

In the present study the investigator has tried to touch upon a value, a social-biological-political construct which has very complex origins and which is deep rooted in one's consciousness. The effectiveness of such a study cannot be judged merely from statistics. Statistical analysis may or may not show change at conventionally accepted significant level improvement in attitudes, stereotyping or value judgement; it is an inadequate tool to evaluate the subtle nuances of the reasoning and justifications and the complex thought process behind value judgements. Even if statistical analysis shows a significant difference, the change could be short-lived. The achievement of the programme, however, lies in that the discussions have shaken absolute and uncritical acceptance of the *status quo* of at least some students. The ideas and questions planted by the programme may remain dormant for a long time but may spark off when the adolescents would face a gender related value-conflict in future. They may decide to question the so-far-taken-for-granted gender bias and a changed frame of mind may make them more receptive to the idea of gender equality in future. Even a small number of such adolescents could have considerable impact in their families and peer groups.

Relevance of the Programme to Adolescents

Another achievement of the programme is that it gave an opportunity to adolescent boys and girls to discuss issues which were very close to their hearts (as suggested by their comments during the pretesting). The rigid school curriculum never gives them a chance for such discussions. It is very reassuring for an adolescent girl to realise that many girls and women resent gender bias faced in day-to-day situations and she is not abnormal in her feelings. It is equally reassuring for a boy to find out that it is not abnormal if his interests fall in the so called 'feminine' domain. Besides, heterosexual relationships are a crucial aspect in gender issues. It was an important step ahead for the boys and girls participating in the experiment when a crack was made in the segregation forced by the rigid classroom environment. They began to share ideas, listen to and argue and discuss with the other gender. Thus the key factors of the new communication paradigm — participation, sharing and analysis — seem to have played a role in these sessions.

The programme using Value Discussion Approach for Gender Equality throughout conveyed a subtle message that there is not always 'only one' way to respond to a situation and yet ethics and democratic values are not simply a matter of personal taste or preference. Students also learnt that reasoning and clear presentation of one's thoughts are important skills for persuading others.

The programme also exposed students to various options, choices and life-styles other than their own. For example, while presenting the dilemma about change of surname after marriage the investigator suggested as a possible option that husband takes on wife's surname or both use two surnames with a hyphen. It brought about laughter and loud chuckles from the class. Many students thought that the investigator was cracking a joke. Later, when she gave them the example of the well known economist-journalist Swaminathan Ankalesaria Aiyar, they were very surprised. The name of course was not familiar to them. But after the discussion was over, a sizeable number of students (about 20) opted for the choice that both, husband and wife, should use two surnames with a hyphen. Similarly, when the pretest on gender-stereotyping with respect to professions was given, there were several professions like chef, architect, baby-sitter, entrepreneur etc. about which students had very little awareness. The list of 50 professions struck them with realization that there are so many professional options other than doctor, engineer, lawyer and teacher.

Housework as a Profession

Housework which was considered predominantly feminine before treatment (only 14.6% of the respondents considering it appropriate for both genders and 70.2% considering it appropriate only for women), became acceptable as appropriate for both genders to 38% of the respondents and only 43.3% considered it appropriate for only women. Here one can see that even though Housework as profession was retained in the category 'predominantly feminine' even after the treatment, the numbers of acceptors and rejectors of gender-bias changed remarkably in favour of gender-equality.

This change of stereotyping with respect to Housework as profession deserves special attention; for centuries women have not been able to leave home for outside work as housework has been considered as women's domain and this leaves no time and opportunity to women to show off their ability in other professions. The load of housework may be considered the single most significant factor which has so far come in the way of women going for professions considered domain of men. Even when women go for outside work, it is usually at the lower levels only as the demands of housework do not allow them to accept higher positions which would require them to remain away from home even after the usual office hours.

Stereotyping with respect to the professions of Baby-sitter, Nurse and Pre-school Teacher has not been as much affected as Housework as these professions, especially Baby-sitter and Pre-school Teacher, deal with small children for whom men are not considered capable at all for these jobs. Here the gender-bias is acting against men, but still it leaves women at a disadvantage.

It is interesting to note that when it comes to accounting innate qualities as the reason for accepting a profession as predominantly masculine or feminine, the treatment did not show positive influence in changing a deep-rooted gender-bias.

Each dilemma touched one relatively simple issue to begin with, but in the process of discussion several interconnected issues got explored. For example, the Dilemma-10 posed a conflict about a couple. The young man and the woman were co-students and later got married. The woman does not want to wear everyday all the wedding symbols like *Mangalsutra, Bindi* and *Sindoor* which her husband wants her to because of the tradition in his convention-bound family. The discussion in its logical flow touched upon various aspects like individual freedom and social norms... why only women are required to wear wedding symbols and change so much ... why husband's parents have the right to control the daughter-in-law's personal conduct and day-to-day life whereas a wife's parents cannot say anything to the son-in-law ... could that be one reason why parents prefer sons? The same goes for income: in-laws have the right to use a woman's income and her parents who have educated her have no claim on her income or her husband's income. Is that why parents are not interested in daughter's career and professional education? Is that the motivation for amniocentesis?

The discussion sessions also gave students an idea that gender issues do not exist in isolation but are a part of interconnected, simultaneously operating forces.

Influence of Television and Films

How far the public behaviour is influenced by films and TV has been under debate long since. Whatever the final conclusion in this debate, the observations in this study with respect to the professions of Collector and Police Officer are interesting. The profession of Police Officer was considered appropriate for both genders before treatment but that of Collector was considered more appropriate for men, even though, objectively speaking, the Police Officer may have to face greater hazards than the Collector. Here a plausible explanation is that TV serials like *Udan* and high media profile of Police Officers like Ms Kiran Bedi have influenced public opinion to accept Police Officer's job appropriate for both genders. After the treatment there was a remarkable shift in case of Collector as profession. Compared to 58.6% of respondents considering it appropriate for both and 21.76% considering it appropriate for men only before treatment, 83.6% of the respondents considered it appropriate for both genders and the percentage considering it appropriate for men only was reduced to zero!

Influence of Independent Variables

Sex of the respondent, Profession of Mother, Education of Mother, Education of Father, and type of family did not significantly influence the effect of the treatment, with respect to attitude towards Gender Equality, Gender-Stereotyping and Value-Judgement; Profession of father did not have significant influence on gender-stereotyping or value judgement; it influenced Attitude only, but considering the overall impact of the treatment, attitude was not significantly affected.

One may, therefore, logically conclude that Value-Discussion Model as a treatment in communication to promote gender equality works without being influenced by variables considered in the present experiment. The present study, however, by its very nature is a relatively short-term and small-size project. It would be a good idea to carry on experiments and observations on the lines of the present study on a larger scale which may give better insight into the influence of the independent variables included in the present study.

Mother's profession does not appear to influence attitude towards gender equality (as shown by statistical analysis), but Father's profession does show significant influence on this attitude. Logically one may guess that it is Mother's profession which should influence attitude towards gender equality in a patriarchal set-up but here the situation we find is quite the opposite of our expectation. Probably this statistical result is due to the relatively small number of mothers (in the sample) who were working women (5 working mothers as opposed to 60 working fathers).

The positions taken by boys and girls on the twelve situations for the value test and the reasons given by them in support of their choices indicate that girls are as much gender-biased as boys. Similar observation was made during the group discussions following the dilemma presentations in the classroom. This point has to be noted while considering the weight of the argument that gender-bias will decrease if greater number of women occupy decision-making positions. This is especially applicable to media when people argue that the image of women in media will change in positive direction if there are more women communicators. The present study clearly shows that both, boys and girls, need gender sensitivity programmes.

EDUCATIONAL IMPLICATIONS

1. Adolescent boys and girls find Value Discussion Approach interesting and useful in exploring gender issues. Schools may try to include value discussion sessions in their class-rooms and also in co-curricular programmes. Value Discussion Model may also be used for promoting other democratic values in adolescents.
2. Stereotypes and attitudes do not take place in vacuum. They are shaped and reinforced by constantly repeated verbal and visual images. Schools and media should make optimum efforts to expose students to images that counteract the gender-stereotyping reinforced by socialization at home and in society-at-large.
3. The Value-Discussion Model after further research could also be used in gender-sensitization programmes for parents, teachers, and administrators and policy planners. Parent-Teacher Associations could be an appropriate platform.
4. For wider educational application, the Value-Discussion Model could be adapted for mass media like newspapers, radio and television to generate greater awareness and extensive discussion about gender issues.

3. Further research on the Value Discussion Model should explore its effectiveness with different groups such as parents, teachers, administrators and policy makers.

CONCLUSION

Gender equality is an enormously complex concept but an essential value for a democratic set-up which India has chosen. Biological factors do and will continue to play their role in shaping gender differences but it is imperative to recognize the important role of socio-cultural factors which are continuously and at present very rapidly changing as a result of technological advances. Gender role-sharing seems to be an alternative worth exploring to replace rigid gender role-stereotyping or role reversal. Younger generation needs be sensitized on gender issues through appropriate communication and educational approaches. Value Discussion Model appears to be an appropriate tool for this task as shown by the present study.

Presently most of the discussions, seminars and programmes on gender issues are confined to groups who are already supporters of the idea of gender equality. Instead of 'preaching the converts', it is now time to place emphasis on reaching the groups unexposed to the idea.

APPENDICES

APPENDIX 1

SELF-ADMINISTERED QUESTIONNAIRE
BACKGROUND INFORMATION

Roll No.______

1. Name of the School ______________________________

2. Name ______________________________
   (If you do not want to givc your name you can leave this item)

3. Male/Female ______________________________

4. Education of Mother ______________________________
   (Please give details like level, subject etc.) ______________________________

5. Education of Father ______________________________
   (Please give details)

6. Profession of Mother ______________________________
   (Please give details like place of work, designation etc.) ______________________________

7. Profession of Father ______________________________
   (Please give details) ______________________________

8. Type of Family Joint / Nuclear

APPENDIX 2

ATTITUDE SCALE

Instruction

These days there is a lot of discussion going on about equality between men and women. Given below are several statements pertaining to equality between men and women. Against each statement are given five options. Please read each statement very carefully and mark ✓ for the option which reflects how you feel about the statement. There is no right or wrong answer. Please be honest in expressing your response.

Statement	Fully Agree	Agree	Undecided	Disagree	Fully disagree
1. The whole idea of gender equality is ridiculous because women are naturally inferior to men.					
2. The Gender Equality Movement is a ploy of women to snatch power from men.					
3. Gender equality is beneficial to both, men and women.					
4. There should be clearcut and separate roles for men and women in society.					
5. Gender equality in society would give better chance to individuals to pursue their					

Statement	Fully Agree	Agree	Un-decided	Dis-agree	Fully disagree
interests, without social pressure.					
6. There is no need to question the appropriateness of existing gender bias in our society.					
7. Men are superior to women as can be seen in all religious texts.					
8. Gender equality is a dangerous notion as it will lead to divorce and broken families.					
9. If women want equality they should forsake benefits like maternity leave.					
10. Government should design policies that would enhance gender equality in our country.					
11. Working towards gender equality is a sheer waste of time on a useless matter					
12. Men who support the gender equality movement are sissy					
13. If India wants to be a truly democratic country, efforts for gender equality should be given priority.					

Statement	Fully Agree	Agree	Un-decided	Dis-agree	Fully dis-agree
14. Women who believe in gender equality are man-haters.					
15. No self-respecting man can consider a woman his equal.					
16. If an institution organises an exhibition or a programme on gender equality, I would like to participate as a volunteer.					
17. Gender equality is risky as it would make women aggressive and they will dominate over men.					
18. Gender equality will help men strike a healthy balance between public and private life.					
19. Gender equality will help women strike a healthy balance between public and private life.					
20. The present patriarchal system is perfectly fine — no need to change it.					
21. Gender equality is not feasible because men are naturally unjust and have a tendency to exploit.					

Statement	Fully Agree	Agree	Un-decided	Dis-agree	Fully dis-agree
22. If women want gender equality they should stop being sensitive and caring.					
23. In a fund-raising campaign for gender equality, I would like to donate money.					
24. One way to bring gender equality is to oppress men because they oppressed women in the past.					
25. Media should give positive and wide coverage to gender equality.					
26. Upbringing of children would be better in a family believing in gender equality.					

GENDER STEREOTYPE TEST

Professions

Given below is a list of various professions. If, according to you, a profession is appropriate only for women, please mark ✓ in the box under the title "Appropriate for Women". If you feel that a profession is appropriate only for men, please mark ✓ in the box under the heading "Appropriate for Men". Please also give reasons for your answer. If, according to you, a profession is appropriate for both men and women, please mark ✓ in both the boxes.

Profession	Appropriate for Women	Appropriate for Men	Reason/ Comments
1. Doctor			
2. Nurse			
3. Actor			
4. Lawyer			
5. Dress Designer			
6. Secretary			
7. Typist			
8. Baby Sitter			
9. Chef			
10. Pilot			
11. Pre-school Teacher			
12. University Teacher			
13. Bank Teller			
14. Manager			

Profession	Appropriate for Women	Appropriate for Men	Reason/ Comments
15. Taxi Driver			
16. Computer Engineer			
17. Police Officer			
18. Collector			
19. Accountant			
20. Waiter			
21. Fashion Model			
22. Sales Person			
23. Politician			
24. Minister			
25 Industrialist			
26. Person engaged in household work			
27. Shopkeeper			
28. Architect			
29. Photographer			
30. Musician			
31. Dancer			
32. Farmer			
33. Film Producer			
34. Film Director			
35. Social Worker			
36. Announcer			
37. Librarian			
38. Telephone Operator			
39. Receptionist			
40. Computer Programmer			
41. Journalist			
42. Mechanic			
43. Electrician			

Profession	Appropriate for Women	Appropriate for Men	Reason/ Comments
44. Scientist			
45. Mathematician			
46. Linguist			
47. Advertising Executive			
48. Sports Person			
49. Finance and Tax Consultant			
50. Corporate Officer			

APPENDIX 4

VALUE TEST ON GENDER EQUALITY

Given below are twelve situations. Situations like these occur often in our daily life. You have to say what you would do if you happen to be in a similar situation and then give the reason for your answer. Under every situation four alternatives are given. If you choose one of the first three alternative indicate (✓) against your choice. The fourth alternative is to suggest an option which is different from the given alternatives. After you have made a choice please give reasons for your choice.

I. You have gone for mountaineering with your friends. After reaching your destination you come to know that the organisers have not hired a cook. The organisers argue that in the group there are many girls who can cook after completing the day's mountaineering which would help cut down the expenditure and the group members will have to pay less per head.

(1) You agree with the organisers and you will support them.

(2) You do not agree with the organisers but you will keep quiet. You would quietly slip away when the work is being distributed.

(3) You do not agree with the organisers and you will openly oppose their decision.

(4) Any other option (Please specify).

II. Your younger brother has just passed his H.S.C. examination with good marks. He wants to join the Home Science College but the College refuses to accept boys. Your brother wants to take action against such a policy but does not receive much support at home or from friends. Under the circumstances:

(1) You will tell your brother that his choice is inappropriate and will advise him to choose some other discipline.

(2) You do not mind your brother's choice but you will not involve yourself in his crusade against the College.

(3) You support your brother's choice and will help him take action against the College.

(4) Any other option (Please specify).

III. You live with your parents and two elder brothers. One of your brothers is married. He and your *bhabhi* (sister-in-law) work in the same office. They have an infant daughter. Your *bhabhi* does the household work before leaving for office and also cooks dinner after she comes back. She expects that your brother should share the childcare and household responsibilities but your parents do not like this at all as they think men are not expected to attend to such work.

(1) You believe your parents' stand is appropriate and you will support them.

(2) You agree with your *bhabhi* but will keep quiet in the matter.

(3) You will take your *bhabhi*'s side and try to convince your parents that your *bhabhi*'s expectations are reasonable.

(4) Any other option (Please specify).

IV. Your parents have gone out leaving the charge of the house with you. In the evening some guests drop in. You have to carry on conversation with the guests. Your younger sister is doing her home-work while your younger brother is watching television. Whom would you ask to prepare tea and offer snacks to the guests?

(1) Ask your younger sister :

(2) Ask your younger brother

(3) You will not offer tea or snacks to the guests under the pretext that parents are not at home.

(4) Any other option (Please specify).

V. You live in a joint family. In your family there is a tradition that after coming back from school girls have to help in household work while boys go out to play.

(1) You will oppose the tradition and will try to change it (how?)

(2) You do not like the tradition but you will keep quiet about it.

(3) You do not find anything wrong with the tradition and will let it continue.

(4) Any other option (Please specify).

VI. Your elder sister is a very bright student. She graduated this year and she has been engaged to a graduate young man from your community. Your sister desires to study for a post-graduate degree but the boy's family is not in favour of it. If your sister studies further the betrothal may be terminated. Under the circumstances:

(1) You will support your sister's wish for further studies.

(2) You will persuade your sister to take-up something like tailoring or dress-design instead of going for a Master's degree.

(3) You will persuade your sister to abandon the idea of studying further and get married.

(4) Any other option (Please specify).

VII. You are a member of the Youth Club of your community. The Club has planned to organise summer vacation courses for members. With a large majority it has been decided to conduct Cookery classes for girls and Karate classes for boys. Parents also whole-heartedly support the plan.

(1) You agree with the Club's plan.

(2) You do not agree with the Club's plan and will be vocal about it and demand that boys and girls should be allowed to join any class that interests them.

(3) You do not agree with the Club's plan but you will not take a stand against it.

(4) Any other option (Please specify).

VIII. Your elder brother has recently got married. Your *bhabhi* likes to wear Salwar-Kameez, midi-skirt etc. which are in current fashion. In your family daughters are allowed to wear such dresses but the daughter-in-law is supposed to wear only the traditional Sari. The elders in the family are very strict about the dress code. Under the circumstances :

(1) You will support the elders.

(2) You feel that the elders are being unfair but would prefer to keep quiet.

(3) You will take your *bhabhi*'s side and pressurise the elders to change.

(4) Any other option (Please specify).

IX. A group of boys and girls in your class planned mischief against a new teacher but got caught. You are not in this group. The Principal gives very harsh punishment to the boys in the group but gives just a verbal scolding to the girls.

(1) You do not agree with the Principal's action but since you are not a part of the group you will keep quiet.

(2) You will openly say that the action is unjust and oppose it.

(3) You agree with the Principal's action.

(4) Any other option (Please specify).

X. You are a member of a youth organization which decides to launch a crusade against social evils. A procession is planned to generate social awareness against dowry and violence against women. The procession is going to pass through your neighbourhood. Your past experience has shown that if you participate in the procession your neighbours are going to ridicule you later. Many of them have taken dowry so it is quite likely that relations with them could get strained. Under the circumstances :

(1) You will persuade your youth members to cancel the procession.

(2) You will participate in the procession.

(3) You will not try to stop the procession but at the last minute will find an excuse to slip away.

(4) Any other option (Please specify).

XI. In Mumbai, they run special "Women's Trains" at the time when most offices finish work. There is a proposal for Women's Bus on similar lines in your city. The decision about the proposal will be taken by referendum. In your family there is no working woman.

(1) You will vote for the women's bus.

(2) You will vote against the women's bus.

(3) You will not vote.

(4) Any other option (Please specify)

XII. You support gender equality and therefore you frequently become a victim of jabs and ridicule. Sometimes you have to face strong opposition in your family and peer group and at times you also get scolded for advocating gender equality.

(1) You will change your value for gender equality because it creates problems for you.

(2) You will stick to your value but in future you will be careful that your value for gender equality is not reflected in your public utterances or behaviour.

(3) You will stick to your value and continue to think and behave the way you do now.

(4) Any other option (Please specify).

APPENDIX 5

PROCEEDINGS OF VALUE DISCUSSION SESSIONS

Detailed record of the presentation and proceedings of all the 16 Value Discussion Sessions was maintained by the investigator. The record contains the theme of the dilemma, mode of presentation, day, date and time, prediscussion response of the group, arguments presented by each group, counter arguments by students, probe-questions by the investigator and the post-discussion response of the group. Observations regarding the class environment and students' behaviour were also recorded. The investigator took down important points during the sessions. Besides, all the small groups put down their arguments in writing and submitted the papers to the investigator. The prediscussion and post-discussion choices were put down on slips of papers and willing students also expressed them verbally in the class.

Three samples of the proceedings of the Value Discussion Sessions are presented here.

Sample 1

Date	: October 30, 1993
Day	: Saturday
Time	: 7.30 a.m. to 9.15 a.m.
Presentation	: Story-telling with large photographs (cut-out from calenders) used like flash-cards.
Theme	: This is Rupa. The photograph shows her wedding ceremony. Here are her parents and here is the bridegroom. Rupa feels that even after her marriage, she should be given an equal share in her parents' property. The second photograph shows Rupa's two brothers who do not like the idea of Rupa getting an equal share in parents' property.

Q. What should Rupa's parents do?

(1) Give Rupa an equal share.
(2) Divide the property only among the two brothers.
(3) Any other option.

Pre-discussion voting showed 34 students supporting the idea that Rupa should get an equal share in the property. There were only ten girls in this group.

The second group of 20 students — all girls — said that a married daughter should not have any claim on the parents' property.

Both these groups were further divided into smaller groups of five to six students. Each small group then worked on their own for about 40 minutes and put down the collective arguments on paper.

Arguments Presented in Favour of Position-1 (Rupa should get equal share in parents' property)

1. Those who believe in equality between men and women, should support girls getting equal right to property.
2. It is commonly argued that parents spend a lot on girls' education and wedding so there is no need to give them a share in property. But, parents spend on boys' education and wedding too. It has nothing to do with property rights.
3. Expenditure on wedding is parents' own personal choice. If they want, they can spend less. Moreover, boys spend parental money on various things — sometimes on vices, sometimes just to have some fun.
4. Times have changed today so we must change. Not giving property to girls is an injustice.
5. People say that after marriage a girl has to go and live with her husband's family but it is not her fault, and anyway, girls did not design this convention.
6. Right to parental property would give great support to a girl if in future she lands into trouble. For example, economic crisis in her family, disability or death of her husband or divorce. After death of her parents she will not have to be economically dependent and face humiliation.

It is brothers' duty to spend money for sisters' welfare. They should not shirk their responsibility even if girls receive equal share in property.

Arguments Presented in Favour of Position- 2

(Parents should divide the property only among two brothers)

1. Parents have to spend a lot on a daughter. First of all on education, then on professional training and after that on wedding. They have to give her utensils and furniture to set up her home. Besides, girls have to be given dowry. After spending so much of money, how can a daughter demand property?
2. Parents spend a lot of money on daughter's education but they do not get anything from her income. Her in-laws get benefit from her income. A girl should understand this, demand a share in her in-law's property and should not put her parents and brothers in economic crisis.
3. It is our Indian tradition that once a woman is married, her husband and not her parents, has to look after her.
4. Parents have no right on daughter after marriage so what right has she on their property? Even when they are ill or in trouble, the sons and daughters-in-law are going to take care of them.
5. Property rights to girls will be treated as a kind of a dowry under a different name. It will actually have negative consequences for girls.
6. Parents always marry their daughters into superior and financially better-off families. So daughters do not need parents' property.
7. If a girl from financially poor family claims property right her brothers and parents would have to starve. A girl would have her husband to support her but her brother has to support his wife, children and parents. Girls who claim parental property would be a great burden for their parents.

Probe Questions by the Investigator

(1) Is it really so that girls always get married into superior and financially better-off families?

(2) Some of you argue that if girls have equal right on parental property, boys would prefer to marry girls only from families with good property. It will have negative consequences. On the other hand, you seem to support the practice that girls be married into financially stronger families. Isn't it equally unjust for boys who are good but from poor families?

(3) When girls have equal right to parental property, should parents expect married daughters to support the family of origin?

(4) Many of you stated that parents have no right on daughters after they are married nor can they get the benefit of daughter's income. Do you support these conventions?

(5) Is it possible to evolve more need-based flexible system of inheritance?

Sample 2

Date	: October 1, 1993
Day	: Friday
Time	: 2.30 p.m. to 4.30 p.m.
Presentation	: Film clip recorded on video.
Theme	: The film clip is taken from the Hindi film "Andhi" directed by Gulzar and starring Sanjeev Kumar as J.K., Suchitra Sen as Aarti and Rehman as Aarti's father. Aarti's father is a leading political figure. Aarti has married J.K., a hotel manager despite her father's opposition. The scene on video begins with Aarti and J.K. in morning at their home in a happy mood. J.K. is photographing Aarti when she gets up and begins to get ready to go out. As she takes out a Khaddar Sari, J.K. senses that she plans to go for a political meeting with her father. J.K. objects, harshly and tells Aarti to stay at home and

look after home and their daughter. Aarti says that sometimes when she has to go, he can take leave from work and look after their daughter. J.K. does not agree and tells Aarti to stop *Netagiri* (leadership).

Later when Aarti goes to meet her father, he is very upset. He had encouraged Aarti to acquire a higher degree in law and become a barrister so that she had a bright future ahead. Now he feels, she is putting everything at stake for a lowly hotel manager. She should not sacrifice her political ambition and career for him.

Q. What should Aarti do?

(1) Sacrifice her political career and ambition.

(2) Go ahead in politics and not waste her talent and education.

(3) Find any other option.

Pre-discussion voting showed 28 students — all boys — opting for the position 1 whereas 3 students — 2 boys and 1 girl — opted for the position 2. A group of 18 students — 15 girls and 3 boys — said that they did not agree with either and would like to find some other option.

The first and the third group divided themselves into smaller groups to work out arguments in support of their position and discussed for about 50 minutes.

Arguments Presented in Favour of Position-1
(Aarti should sacrifice her political career and ambition)

(1) If Aarti had listened to her father and had not married J.K. she could have fulfilled her ambition but she never listened to him. Now that she is married she should obey her husband.

(2) Once a woman gets married, she has all kinds of restrictions (*Lagna pachhi stri saat feraa naa atut bandhanmaa bandhai*

jaay chhe). When she becomes mother she has added responsibilities (*Maanu mamtabharyu mahaan roop dhaaran kare chhe*). Aarti has to obey her husband's wishes and look after her child. Failing this her children will not get proper love and care and may later become anti-social elements. Instead, Aarti should concentrate on developing her child into a good leader and fulfil her ambitions through her child.

(3) A young child needs mother. Only mother can form good habits in children (*Baalakne maataa-j sanskaar aapi shake*).

(4) If Aarti wanted to join politics and become a leader, why did she get married? She should have remained single.

(5) Aarti's husband has a good job with good income. Why should Aarti work?

(6) How long can Aarti's husband keep on taking leave? After all, a home is home because of woman (*ghar to stri vagar shobhe-j nahin*). Family should be her first priority.

(7) Aarti can stay at home, look after her child and do some other work like dress making, embroidery etc. if she wants to earn.

(8) A woman should never have political ambitions. It brings bad name to her and her entire family (*badnaami thaay chhe*).

Arguments Presented in Favour of Position-2
(Aarti should go ahead in politics)

(1) Aarti's father has spent so much money on her education. She has acquired higher degrees. If she becomes a leader, she will have plenty of money. She can keep a good governess for the child. Hiring a governess will resolve the entire conflict.

(2) The child's grandparents can look after her.

Arguments Presented in Favour of Position-3
(Any other option)

(1) Aarti's husband is right in a way and her father is also right in a way. Aarti can balance her time between work and home in such

a way that her child receives adequate care and love. If her husband gives her full co-operation, this is possible.

(2) Aarti should work but the rest of the time she should concentrate on her daughter. This way she can fulfil her ambition and can also please her husband.

(3) Child is not only mother's responsibility. Father too, has to share this responsibility. If Aarti has an important meeting, her husband should take leave. He should also help her with other household chores. Then Aarti can certainly manage home and career. She should not waste her talents and education.

(4) Husband and wife should compromise and find a mutually acceptable solution because it is very bad for children if parents keep fighting.

(5) If a man continues to work after marriage, why can't a woman?

(6) Husband and wife dream many dreams together. If wife also earns they can fulfil these dreams. So an educated woman should utilise her education and earn. At the same time she should not neglect her child and home by over-concentrating on her career.

Questions by the Groups to one another

(1) Can hiring a governess solve all the problems?

(2) Is it fair to fulfil one's ambitions through one's child? Aarti has a daughter. If Aarti implants her ambition for a political career in her daughter, would not the daughter face the same problems when she grows up?

(3) Your group said that if a woman entered politics she would get a bad reputation. Should we young people support such social conventions or fight them?

Probe Questions by the Investigator

(1) Some of you say that if a woman wants to be a political leader she should not get married. Would you suggest the same for a man?

The answer was 'No'.

Why? (This question led to a long discussion on how we expect much more from a woman as wife, mother and daughter-in-law compared to a man.)

(2). You said that a young child needs lots of love and care. Very true. Can only mother give these or also father? Anyone else?

(3) Would Aarti want to work for any reason/motive other than supplementing the family income?

(4) Some of you suggested that if Aarti is keen on working she could take up dress designing or embroidery and work at home. You know she has studied law — she is a barrister. Would a lawyer, say for example a male lawyer, like to do that? Would a lawyer have the necessary skill, interest and aptitude to take up dress designing/embroidery professionally?

(5) A large number of you said that Aarti should go ahead with her political career and also look after her family and home. Would Aarti have enough time and energy for both? Would that mean no time to relax? What could help her balance home and career? Or alternatively can you suggest a way to Aarti to balance home and career?

(6) Are grandparents always free or able or willing to look after children? What if they have their own career? (It took sometime for students to accept the idea that a grandmother could have her own career.)

Sample 3

Date	:	September 11, 1993
Day	:	Saturday
Time	:	9.30 a.m. to 11.00 a.m.
Presentation	:	Oral presentation with line drawing on the blackboard.
Theme	:	Mira is a bank officer earning a very good salary. She meets Sanjeev. Sanjeev earns much less than Mira does but he is intelligent

and also a very mature, good natured person. Mira and Sanjeev fall in love and they want to get married. Mira's parents oppose the idea of marriage whereas her sister advises her to go ahead.

Q. What should Mira do?

(1) Marry Sanjeev.

(2) Listen to her parents' advice and not marry Sanjeev.

(3) Any other option.

Pre-discussion voting showed 35 students in favour of position-1 which supported the marriage, 16 students voted for position-2 which did not support the marriage. None of the students voted for any other option.

Group 1 was divided into six small groups and Group 2 into three small groups for small group discussion.

Arguments Presented in Favour of Position-1
(Mira should marry Sanjeev)

(1) Boys accept girls who earn less than themselves than why not the reverse?

(2) Certain professions like teaching do not pay well but that does not mean the person is inferior.

(3) Mira is a career woman. If she marries a boy who earns a very high salary, he may not allow her to work after their marriage because her income will not be necessary.

(4) *Miyan-beebee raaji to kyaa karegaa kaazi?*

(5) Personal qualities of the boy are more important than his income. The important thing is that Sanjeev has no vices, no addictions.

(6) If Mira is ready to compromise on certain luxuries, there will not be any problem. If Sanjeev's income is very low, Mira can continue working but only if her husband consents.

(7) If Sanjeev is bright and good in his work, he will rise in future.

(8) Love and peace between husband and wife are more important

than money. Marrying a person of one's choice means more chances of marital success.

(9) If Mira and Sanjeev have confidence in themselves and trust each other, income will be a trivial issue.

Arguments Presented in Favour of Position-2 (Mira should listen to her parents' advice and not marry Sanjeev)

(1) In future, Sanjeev will suffer from inferiority complex. He will be jealous of Mira and there will be problems in their married life.

(2) Mira and Sanjeev will not be socially acceptable as couple. They will be victim of societal criticism and taunting from relatives which in turn will cause problems in their marriage.

(3) The marriage will diminish the reputation of Mira's parents in society.

(4) In affairs like marriage girls should listen to their parents. Parents' advice is always for the good of children.

Probe Questions by the Investigator

(1) When a girl's husband earns higher salary she feels very proud but when a wife earns higher salary, there are all kinds of problems (as dicussed by you). What could be the reasons? (How do you explain this situation?)

(2) One group says that if Sanjeev's income is very low Mira can continue working. Do you suggest that she should leave work if Sanjeev has a reasonably good income?

(3) You also say that Mira can continue working but only if her husband consents. Why?

APPENDIX 6

DILEMMA - 1

ORAL PRESENTATION WITH LINE DRAWINGS ON THE BLACK-BOARD

Situation	Options	Response	
		Pre-discussion choice	Post-discussion choice
The Shah family is a family of six. Ramanbhai and Sushilabahen have two sons, Sanjay and Sameer, and two daughters, Swati and Shruti. All the four children are adolescents. Ramanbhai's parents — Manibahen and Bachubhai — also live with them.	(1) Parents should listen to girls	40 (8 boys)	
	(2) Parents should listen to grandparents	12 (2 girls)	
Sanjay and Sameer are allowed all sorts of freedom — use of car, late nights, mixed company, out-of-station picnics . . . Swati and Shruti have restrictions, like be back before 7.00 in the evening, no out-station picnics or mixed parties etc.	(3) Any other option (a compromise was suggested — No too many restricitons but not too much freedom or misuse of freedom — applicable to both, boys and girls)	9	When this group finished arguing the boy who presented the arguments wrote (3) on the black-board, marked an emphatic ✔ on it and the class

(Contd.)

DILEMMA - 1 : *(Contd.)*

Situation	Options	Resopnse	
		Pre-discussion choice	Post-discussion choice
Both the girls demand equal freedom but grand-parents point out that for girls, good reputation in society is very important, especially from point of view of marriage. It is better to keep girls under vigil. Q. Whom should the parents listen to? (1) Girls (2) Grandparents (3) Any other option			clapped enthusiastically.

Note : The number of total students for pre- and post-discussion response may differ because not necessarily all students responded.

DILEMMA - 2

Oral presentation with flash-cards

Situation	Response	
	Pre-discussion	Post-discussion
You are a member of the legislative assembly. At present all the girls in Gujarat get free education at all levels. There is going to be a fresh debate in assembly over the issue and your opinion is crucial.		
Q. What will you do?		
Options		
(1) Support free education for girls	39 (10 boys)	1
(2) Oppose free education for girls	12 (2 girls)	2
(3) Any other option : Free education to poor boys and girls		37

DILEMMA - 3

Oral presentation with line drawing on the black-board

Situation	Response	
	Pre-discussion	Post-discussion
Mira is a bank officer earning a very good salary. She meets Sanjeev. Sanjeev earns much less than Mira but he is intelligent and also a very mature good natured person. Mira and Sanjeev fall in love and want to get married. Mira's parents oppose the idea of marriage whereas her sister advises her to go ahead.		
Q. What should Mira do?		
Options		
(1) Marry Sanjeev	35	45
(2) Listen to her parents' advice and not to marry Sanjeev	16	6
(3) Any other option	—	—

DILEMMA - 4

Role-play enacted by students themselves

Situation	Response	
	Pre-discussion	Post-discussion
In the school's parent-teacher association meeting, one group of parents suggests that girls' uniform needs a change. Skirts and pinafores should go. Instead comfortable shorts and shirts should be introduced. Skirts and frocks restrict free movement during sports and physical activities or games in the recess. They make girls conscious and hamper development. The other group opposes saying that skirts and frocks are more appropriate, graceful and socially desirable.		
Q. What decision should the Principal take? *Options*		
(1) Change the uniform	25 (all girls)	No voting
(2) Not to change the uniform	24 (8 girls)	Very hot discussion, arguments continue till the end
(3) Any other option : Girls can come to school in skirt/ pinafore and change into shorts for P.T./sports	10	

DILEMMA - 5

Story-telling with the help of line drawings

Situation	Response	
	Pre-discussion	Post-discussion
Shaila Desai is a wellknown writer whose books are very popular. She marries Sharad Chauhan, a businessman.		
Q. After her marriage, should Sheila		
(1) Take up Sharad's surname and become Shaila Chauhan?	34	10
(2) Retain her own surname?	18	1
(3) Any other option (e.g. Sharad should take up Shaila's surname or both should write a combined surname like Desai-Chauhan or Chauhan-Desai or only Shaila should write combined surname).	-	20 Both should write a combined hyphenated surname like Chauhan-Desai or Desai-Chauhan. (Probe questions played a crucial role.)

DILEMMA - 6

Story-telling with large photographs cut out from calendars used like flash-cards

Situation	Response	
	Pre-discussion	Post-discussion
This is Rupa. The photograph shows her wedding ceremony. Here are her parents and here is the bridegroom. Rupa feels that even after her marriage, She should be given an equal share in her parents property. The second photograph shows Rups's two brothers who do not like the idea of Rupa getting an equal share in the property.		
Q. What should Rupa's parents do?		
(1) Give Rupa an equal share	34 (10 girls!)	35
(2) Divide the property only among the two brothers	20 (all girls!!)	14
(3) Any other option		

DILEMMA - 7

Film clip recorded on video

Situation	Response	
	Pre-discussion	Post-discussion
The film clip is taken from the Hindi film 'Aandhi' directed by Gulzar and starring Sanjeev Kumar as J.K., Suchitra Sen as Aarti and Rehman as Aarti's father. Aarti's father is a leading political figure. Aarti has married J.K., a hotel manager despite her father's opposition. The scene on video begins with Aarti and J.K. in morning, at their home in a happy mood. J.K. is photographing Aarti when she gets up and begins to get ready to go out. As she takes out a Khaddar Sari, J.K. senses that she plans to go for a political meeting with her father. J.K. objects and harshly tells Aarti to stay at home and look after home and their daughter. Aarti says that sometimes when she has to go, he can take leave from work and look after the daughter. J.K. does not agree and tells Aarti to stop *'Netagiri'* (leadership). Later when Aarti goes to meet her father, he is very upset. He feels that he encouraged Aarti to acquire a higher degree in law and become a barrister so that she has a bright future ahead, now she is putting everything at stake for a lowly hotel manager, she should not sacrifice her political ambition and career for him.		
Q. What should Aarti do?		
(1) Sacrifice her political career and ambition	28 (all boys)	23 (all boys)
(2) Go ahead in politics and should not waste her talent and education	3	2
(3) Find any other option : with her husband's full co-operation Aarti can balance her political career with the role of mother	18 (3 boys)	20

DILEMMA - 8

Audio recording supported by oral presentation and black-board

Situation	Response	
	Pre-discussion	Post-discussion
Micronet computers company is a growing software development company. It has made a large profit this year. The Managing Director believes in democratic decision making style so he asks the employees to suggest what should be done with the profit amount. The employees have three different opinions.		
Q. What should the company do?		
(1) The company should declare a good bonus or organise an incentive tour to Shimla or some other hill-station.	22 (all boys)	17
(2) The company should pump-in more money into advertising to increase the market share.	1 (boy)	0
(3) The company should open a creché-cum-daycare centre for young children of the employees	30 (all girls)	30 (A few boys ran away as the bell rang for recess)

DILEMMA - 9

Drama/Skit performed by students of the Faculty of Journalism and Communication of the M S University of Baroda

Situation	Response	
	Pre-discussion	Post-discussion
Arvindbhai has retired from government service with a small pension. His wife Savitabahen has always been a housewife. Elder daughter Parul is a doctor, has been married to a doctor and both are practising in Ahmedabad. Younger daughter Jagruti is unmarried, and about to complete her post-graduate bachelor's degree in Education (B.Ed.). Arvindbhai and Savitabahen has one son Mit, who has just completed his graduation in Commerce and has got admission in a US University for further studies. The university offered him partial scholarship. When Mit breaks the news his parents are taken aback. As their only son, they expect that Mit will take up a job, support the family and help in getting Jagruti married. Mit argues that while he studies, Parul the elder daughter who is a doctor, can support her parents and Jagruti can also work. This results in family conflict.		
Q. What should Mit do?		
(1) Go to USA, leaving the responsibility of parents to his sisters	12	24
(2) Abandon the idea of further studies and look after the family	14	5
(3) Any other option : (a) Mit should come back as soon as possible (b) After coming back to India Mit should repay whatever the sisters have spent on looking after the family. (c) The younger sister should not get married and support the parents till Mit comes back.	19	30

DILEMMA - 10

Oral presentation with puppets

Situation	Response	
	Pre-discussion	Post-discussion
Radha and Ajay were studying together and then got married recently. Radha wants to continue to dress up the way she used to before they got married. Especially, she does not like to wear everyday all the wedding symbols like *Sindoor*, *Bindi* and *Mangalsootra*. Ajay wants her to change because his parents are conventional.		
Q. What should Radha do?		
(1) Change to please her husband and in-laws	25	9
(2) Do what she wants to do	10	15
(3) Any other option : Radha should wear the wedding symbols on special occasions and should not wear dresses which are too tight or too short.	10	19

DILEMMA - 11

Oral presentation with flash-cards

Situation	Response	
	Pre-discussion	Post-discussion
Nandini is studying in Standard 11. She has two brothers. Bharat is in the first year of college and Anil in the 9th standard. Nandini's *nanima* (maternal grandmother) is very ill so her mother has to go and live with her for about a month. Nandini takes up the charge of cooking and managing the house. Soon after, Nandini's principal informs her that she is selected for an exchange programme in which she will get to travel to many States of India.		
Q. What should Nandini do?		
(1) Go for the exchange programme	34	45
(2) Not go because she should look after the home and cook in her mother's absence	20	7
(3) Any other option	—	—

DILEMMA - 12

Presentation with puppets

Situation	Response	
	Pre-discussion	Post-discussion
Manoj is a bright 17-year old boy. He always gets good marks in all subjects but has aptitude for arts, especially dance. He wants to become a dancer and he has just started taking lessons in Kathak. This sparks off conflict in his family. His family is totally against the idea of a boy taking up dancing as a career. Some of his friends too laugh at his idea.		
Q. What should Manoj do?		
(1) Stick to his plan to learn dancing to become a professional	16	19
(2) Abandon dancing	30	11
(3) Any other option : Manoj can continue dancing as a hobby and take up some other career.	5	15

DILEMMA - 13

Role play by journalism and communication students

Situation	Response	
	Pre-discussion	Post-discussion
Minoo and Ashish live and work in Bombay. Minoo delivered a baby girl. She got maternity leave for three months and looked after the baby. Then her mother and Ashish's mother came for a month to help with the baby as Minoo had to resume work. But they cannot stay any longer. Ashish and Minoo would not like to keep their daughter in creche so Ashish approaches his boss and asks for three months paternity leave. His boss first laughs off the matter and then gets angry but Ashish persists.		
Q. What should the Boss do?		
(1) Allow paternity leave to Ashish	16	18
(2) Not allow paternity leave to Ashish	22	12
(3) Any other option	—	Rest did not respond.

DILEMMA - 14

Role-play by students of the group

Situation	Response	
	Pre-discussion	Post-discussion
Mamta is a Gujarati woman. She is a teacher in a college. Avanish, a Maharashtrian, is also teaching in the same college. They decide to get married and parents of both are happy with their decision. After marriage Mamta lives with her husband and his family. Avanish's family has non-vegetarian eating habits while Mamta is a staunch vegetarian. Her in-laws prefer that she gradually develops the taste for non-veg food. Even if she does not eat she must learn how to cook non-veg food. Mamta is ethically against non-vegetarian eating.		
Q. What should Mamta do?		
(1) Forget her principles and adopt her in-laws's eating habits	16 (10 girls)	10
(2) Stick to vegetarian food and refuse to cook non-veg food	10	12
(3) Stick to vegetarian food but learn to cook non-veg food	21	23

DILEMMA - 15

Video Recording

Situation	Response	
	Pre-discussion	Post-discussion
Sarla is an officer in a big company where Seema has just joined as her assistant. One day Sarla finds Seema very upset. Seema confides that a male officer has been making passes at her. He also writes vulgar letters. Sarla thinks Seema should at once report it to their boss. But Seema hesitates. When she complained about it at home her mother said that it was all Seema's fault as she wore fashionable dresses and has her hair cut. Moreover, her mother felt, complaining to the Boss would malign Seema's reputation and not the male officer's.		
Q. What should Seema do?		
(1) Complain to the Boss	24 (18 boys)	28
(2) Not complain to the Boss	19	9
(3) Any other option : Seema should not wear dresses which exposes her body and if her male colleague repeats his action, she should complain to the boss.	10	16

DILEMMA - 16

Film clip recorded on video

Situation	Response	
	Pre-discussion	Post-discussion
The film clip is taken from the Hindi film 'Abhiman' directed by Hrishikesh Mukherjee and starring Amitabh Bachchan as Amit, Jaya Bhaduri as Sudha and J. Omprakash as a family friend. Amit is a very famous singer. One day on a visit to his village, he hears Sudha singing, falls in love with her and they get married. The scene on the video shows the wedding reception of Amit and Sudha. On the behest of the guests the couple sings a duet. Listening to their singing Omprakash predicts that the alliance is in trouble because Sudha is a much better singer compared to Amit.		
Q. What should Sudha do?		
(1) Continue to sing professionally with Amit	38	43
(2) Should not take up singing as a career	15	7
(3) Any other option	—	—

APPENDIX 7

EXPERT PANNEL FOR EVALUATION OF TOOLS

Prof. Durganand Sinha, ANS Inst. of Social Studies, Patna; Prof. Leela Krishnan, Dept. of Humanities and Social Sciences, Indian Inst. of Technology, Kanpur; Dr. Derek Sequeria, Dr. D.N. Pradhan, Dr. S. Kumar, and Dr. Hemalata Talesara, Faculty of Education and Psychology, The M.S. University of Baroda; Prof. Kalpana Parlikar and Prof. Prerana Mohite, Faculty of Home Science, The M.S. University of Baroda; Mrs. Niti Chopra, Faculty of Journalism and Communication, The M.S. University of Baroda.

Participants in Brainstorming Sessions for Development of Dilemmas

Asha Chaudhari, Mahendra Chauhan, Katyayani Dave, Taruna Khanna, Leena Misra, Ashish Pandya, Gazala Shaikh, Pankaja Sutaria, Jahnavi Contractor, Tejesh Contractor, Seema Pathak, Vihang Pathak, Dr. Milind Sahasrabuddhe, Dr. Sarla Santvani and Dr. Yogini Pathak.

Volunteers Enacting out Dilemmas

Asit Amin, Amit Bhatt, Malavika Bhatt, Dr. Anil Bhatt, Asha Chaudhari, Mahendra Chauhan, Dr. Aparna Dasgupta, Katyayani Dave, Taruna Khanna, Leena Misra, Ashita Mohite, Ishan Pandya, Dr. Mahesh Pandya, Nipa Pandya, Prof. C.H. Pathak, Seema Pathak, Vihang Pathak, Dr. Yogini Pathak, Ajeet Pilo, Prof. Bony Pilo, Rachel Pilo, Mit Raval, Parth Raval, Sarla Santwani, Parul Shah, Gazala Shaikh, Prof. Udaya Shelat, Dr. H.C. Shukul, Savita Shukul, Nidhi Shukul and Gautam Upadhyay.

BIBLIOGRAPHY

Ascroft, J. and Masilela, S. (1989). From Top-down to Coequal Communication: Popular Participation in Development Decision Making (Paper presented at the Seminar on Participation: A Key Concept in Communication and Change) Pune: Univ. of Poona.

Baker, M.A., *et al.* (1980). *Women Today — A Multidisciplinary Approach to Women's Studies.* Monterey, CAL : Brooks/Cole Publ. Co.

Bambawale, Usha (1994). Women's Image as Projected on Screen. *Mainstream,* Feb. 26, 17-20.

Basu, Durgadas (1996). *Shorter Constitution of India.* 12th ed. New Delhi: Prentice-Hall of India.

Bem, Sandral L. (1975). Sex Role Adaptability: One Consequence of Psychological Androgyny. *Jour. Personality and Soc. Psy. 31,* 634-643.

Blokker, W. Glasser, B. and Kirschenbaum, H. (1976) Values Clarification in Health Education. *Health Ed.* April, 1976.

Branon, R. and David, D. (1976). The male sex role: Our culture's blueprint for manhood, and what it's done for us lately. In: D. David and R. Brannon (Eds.), *The Forty-nine Percent majority: The Male Sex Role.* Reading, MA Addison-Wesley.

Campbell, C.V. and Stanley, J.C. (1963). *Experimental and Quasi Experimental Designs for Research on Teaching.* Chicago I L: Gage, Rand McNally.

Caspi, L.L. (1994) The Effect of Strong Women Characters in Literature and the Role of Literature Discussion Groups on the Participation of Sixth-grade students in Literature Discussion Groups and on their Sex-stereotype and Occupational Attitudes .

Ed. D. thesis, University of San Diego, 1994. *Dissertation Abstr, Internat.* 55(12).

Chambers (1972). *Chambers Twentieth Century Dictionary. Bombay*: Allied Publishers.

Chandiram, J. and Agrawal, B. (1982). Towards Equality Women in Indian Television. *Media Asia,* June, 161-64.

Conger, J.J. (1977). *Adolescence and Youth: Psychological Development in a Changing World.* New York: Harper & Row.

Cote-Bonanno, J.F. (1994). Study to determine the impact of Achieving Sex Equity through Students (ASETS). Ph.D. thesis, Seton Hall University, 1994. *Dissertation Abstr. Internat.* 55(5).

Das, R.C. (1987). Education in Values. *Jour. of Indian Ed.* Nov. 1987.

Dewey, J. (1939). *Theory of Valuation*. Chicago: Univ. of Chicago Press.

Diaz-Bordenave, Juan (1989). 'Participative' Communication as a Part of the Building of a Participative Society. Seminar on Participation: A Key Concept in *Communication for Change and Development.* Pune, India. February, 1989.

Edwards, Allen L. (1969). *Techniaues of Attitude Scale Construction*, Bombay: Vakils, Feffer and Simons.

Elkind, D. (1971). *A Sympathetic Understanding of the Child from Six to Sixteen.* Boston: Allyn & Bacon.

Engelber, Elaine A. (1995) Gender Equity and Schools Theory and Practice. Ph D Thesis, Branders University. *Dissertation Abstr. Internat.* 56 (2).

Facione Peter, Scherer, Donald; and Attig, Thomas (1978). *Values and Society: An Introduction to Ethics and Social Philosophy.* Englewood Cliffs, N.J. Prentice-Hall.

Freire, Paulo (1971). *Education for Critical Consciousness.* New York: Continuum.

Freire, Paulo (1972). *Pedagogy of the Oppressed.* Harmondsworth, UK: Penguin.

Gallagher, Margaret (1981). *Uneaual Opportunities: The Case of Women and the Media.* Paris: UNESCO.

Gallagher, Margaret (1983). *The Portrayal and Participation of Women in the Media.* Paris: UNESCO.

Garret, H.E. and Woodworth, R.S. (1961). *Statistics in Psychology and Education.* Bombay: Vakils, Feffer and Remons.

GOI (1974) . *Towards Equality*-Report of the Committee on the Status of Women in India. New Delhi: Dept. of Social Welfare, Ministry of Education and Social Welfare, Government of India.

GOI (1985). *Non-aligned Ministers' Conference on Role of Women in Development.* New Delhi: Author.

GOI (1986). *National Policy on Education.* New Delhi: Dept. of Education, Ministry of Human Resource Development, Government of India.

GOI (1988a). *Mahila Samakhya.* New Delhi: Ministry of Human Resource Development, Govt. of India, Dept. of Education.

GOI (1988b). *The National Perspective Plan for Women, 1988-2000 A.D. — A Perspective for the Women's Movement.* New Delhi: Dept. of Social Welfare, Ministry of Education and Social Welfare, Government of India.

GOI (1992a). *National Policy on Education 1986: Modifications undertaken in 1992.* New Delhi: Ministry of Human Resource Development, Dept. of Education.

GOI (1992b). *Programme of Action (National Policy on Education, 1986.)* New Delhi: Ministry of Human Resource Development, Dept. of Education.

GOI (1994a). *Towards an Enlightened Human Society* (Report of the Committee for Review of National Policy on Education, 1986 - Popularly known as Ramamurti Commission). New Delhi : Ministry of Human Resource Development, Dept. of Education.

GOI (1994b). Country Paper, India — Draft for the 4th World Conference on Women, Beijing, 1995. New Delhi: Dept. of Women and Child Development, Government of India.

GOI (1995). *India 1995 —A Reference Annual.* New Delhi: Publ. Div., Ministry of Information and Broadcasting.

Good, C.V. (1973) *Dictionary of Education.* New York: McGraw Hill.

Gordon, Linda (1991). What's New in Women's History. In: Sneja Gunew (Ed.), *A Reader in Feminist Knowledge*. London, New York: McGraw Hill.

Hersh, R. (1980). *Models of Moral Education.* New York: Longman.

Hirst, Paul (1976). Political Philosophy and Egalitarianism. In Blowers, A. and Thompson. G. (Eds.), *Inequalities Conflict and Change.* Walton Hall: The Open Univ. Press.

Hobster, L.E. (1980). The Effectiveness of Value Clarification Experience for Seventh Grade Students. *Dissertation Abstract Internat.* 41(7).

Joshi, S.R. (1986). Participation of Women in Higher Decision-making Levels of Doordarshan, the Television Authority of India. Paper presented at Cong. of Internat. Assn. for Mass Communication Research, New Delhi.

Kaufman, M.A. (1974). Comparison of a Career Course with Individual Counselling as Facilitators of Vocational Development for College Women. (Unpublished Master's Thesis). Cornell Univ.

Kaul, S. and Ganju, S.C. (1988). Review of Research in Women's Studies Conducted in the M.S. University of Baroda, Baroda. (Addenda 1962-1985). Vadodara: Dept. of Ch. Dev., Fac. of Home Sc., M.S. Univ. of Baroda.

King, M.B. (1995). Teaching for Thinking and Citizenship Education: Examining the Constitution of Student-Citizens in Secondary Social Studies. Ph.D. Thesis, Univ. of Wisconsin, 1994. *Dissertation Abstr. Internat,* 55(11),

Kohlberg, L. and Gilligan, C. (1971). The Adolescent as a Philosopher: The Discovery of the Self in a Post Conventional World. *Daedalus* 100, 1051-1086.

Kolia, Raiza Ahmed. (1995). A Study of Gender Training Programs used Intemationally: A Focus on the African Experience. Ph.D. thesis, University of Ilinois at Urbana-Champaign, 1994. *Dissertation Abstr. Internat.* 55(12).

Krishna Kumar (1986). Growing up Male. *Seminar* No. 318, February, 1986.

Krishnan, Prabha and Dighie, Anita (1989). *Affirmation and Denial: Construction of Femininity on Indian Television.* New Delhi : Sage Publications.

Likert, R. (1932). A technique for the measurement of attitudes. *Arch. Psychol.* No. 140.

Lowe, Marian and Lowe Benston, Margaret (1991). The Uneasy Alliance of Feminism and Academia. In: SNEJA, GUNEW (Ed.), *A Reader in Feminist Knowledge.* London, New York: Routelege.

Makenzie, A.T. (1980) The Curriculum for Similarity Reasoning in High School Students Using Value Clarification and Moral Development Intervenions. *Dissertation Abstr. Internat.* 41(5).

Mc Laren, A.T. (1988). *Gender and Society: Creating a Canadian Woman's Sociology.* Toronto: Copp Clark Pitman.

Melkote, Srinivas R. (1991). *Communication for Development in the Third World: Theory and Practice.* New Delhi: Sage Publications.

Morton (1976). Quoted in H. Kirschenbaum, *Value Clarification.* La Jolla, Ca: Univ. Associates.

Mulvihill, Mary B. (1994). Gender Balancing the Curriculum: Attitudes, Knowledge of Feminist Issues, and Self-Efficacy of Female Undergraduates. Ed. D. Thesis, Fordham Univ. *Dissertation Abstr. Internat.* 55 (11).

Nair, K.S. and White, Shirley (1987). Participatory Message Development: A Conceptual Framework. *Media Development,* 34(3), 36-40.

NCERT (1989). *Training Programme on Methodology of Women's Education and Development—A Handbook.* New Delhi : NCERT, Dept. of Women's Studies.

Nuna, S.C. (1990). *Women and Development.* New Delhi: Nat. Inst. of Ed. Planning and Adm.

Passi, B.K. Goel, D.R. Swarup, S. and Senapati, H. (1986). *Piagetian Teaching Model for Cognitive Development.* (Monograph). Indore: Dept. of Ed., DAVU.

Patric, B.E. (1980). An Action Research Project on Value Clarification: Its Effectiveness on Terminal and Internal Values of Eighth Grader. *Dissertation Abstr. Internat.* 40(l).

Pracejus, E. (1975). The Effect of Value Clarifying on Reading Comprehension. (Unpublished Doctoral Dissertation). Univ. of Pittsburgh.

Raths L.E. (1966). *Values and Teaching*. Columbus, Ohio : Charles E. Merill.

Raths, L.E. *et al.* (1967). *Teaching for Thinking*. Columbus, Ohio: Charles E. Merill.

Rowntree, D.C.A. (1981). *Dictionary of Education*. London: Harper and Row.

Rutkowski, D.M. (1975). The use of value Clarification Strategies in Chemistry Classes to Develop Positive Attitudes Towards Science. (Unpublished Master's Thesis). Oswego, N.Y: State Univ. Coll. of New York.

Shaull, R. (1972) . In *Introduction to Pedagogy of the Oppressed*. Freire, Paulo (Ed.). Harmondsworth, UK: Penguin.

Shaver, J. and Williams, S. (1976). *Facing Value Decision: Rationale Building for Teachers*. Belmont, Calif: Wordsworth.

Short, G. (1993). Sex-typed Behaviour in the Primary School: the significance of Contrasting Explanations. *Educational Research*, 35 (1), Spring.

Singh, A.K. (1988). Comparison of Value Discussion Model with Traditional Arpproach in Terms of Value Clarification of B.Ed. Students. (Unpublished M.Phil. Dissertation) Indore: Sch. of Ed., DAVU.

Singh, A.K. (1991). Comparative Effectiveness of Value Discussion Model with Traditional Approach for Developing Value Clarification of College Students. (Unpublished Doctoral Dissertation) Indore : Sch. of Ed., DAVU.

Singh, P. and Singh, R. (1989). Development of Moral Judgement through Value Analysis Model. *Jour. Ed. & Psy.* 49(1-2).

Smith, M. (1977). *A Practical Guide to Value Clarification*. La Jolla, Calif: Univ. Associates.

Sommers, Christina Hoff (1994). Teaching the Virtues. *SPAN* (35) (1), 10-15; Jan. 1994.

Spence, J.T., Helmreich, R. and Stapp, J. (1975) Ratings of Self and Peers on Sex-role Attributes and their Relation to Self-esteem and Conceptions of Masculinity and Femininity. *Jour. Personality & Soc. Psy.* 32, 29-39.

Steeves, H.L. (1986). Feminism, Communication and Development : Complementary goals in the context of East Africa. Paper presented at Conf. of Internat. Assn. for Mass Communication Res., New Delhi.

Tuckman, B.W. (1972). *Conducting Educational Research.* New York: Harcourt, Brace, Jovanovich.

UGC (1992) *Guidelines for the Development of Women's Studies Programme in Indian Universities and Colleges.* New Delhi: Univ. Grants Commission.

United Nations (1975). *Equal Rights for Women — A Call for Action* (The U.N. Declaration on the Elimination of Discrimination against Women) New York : United Nations.

Verma, A. and Kapadia, S. (1987). A Report of Review of Research in Women's Studies conducted in the Faculty of Home Science, Baroda (1970-1985). Vadodara: Dept. of Ch. Dev., M.S. Univ. of Baroda.

Weiner, Kathleen (1991). Freire and a Feminist Pedagogy of Difference. *Harvard Ed. Review.* 61(4).

Wrightsman, L.S. (1977). *Social Psychology.* Monterey, Calif: Brooks/ Cole Publ. Co.

Young, Cathy (1994). *Man Troubles, Reason.* July, 1994.

Zoonen, Liesbet (1986) . Rethinking Women and the News. Paper presented at Conf. of Internat. Assn. for Mass Communication Research, New Delhi.

INDEX